In *The Fool and the Heretic*, Rob Barrett carefully guides an informed conversation between and among Todd Charles Wood and Darrell R. Falk that results in helpful and constructive dialogue. I learned much from Barrett, Wood, and Falk, and I am sure the same will be true for other readers as well as we all seek to learn how to maintain biblical conviction while practicing genuine kindness toward those with whom we have disagreements about the important theological and ethical issues of our day.

—Dr. David S. Dockery, president, Trinity International University/Trinity Evangelical Divinity School

This book is a rare gem. Nowhere else will you read a conversation like this—an honest dialogue between two Christian biologists who disagree about evolution. They have opposing views on an issue that is deeply important to them, yet they choose to keep talking—because of Christ. This book shows the hard work needed to love one's enemy and seek the unity of believers. This is the authentic dialogue that our churches need today.

—Dr. Deborah Haarsma, president, BioLogos

In an increasingly polarized world, the Christian community often seems as riven with fractious debates as society at large. This wonderful book offers a refreshingly different model of respectful dialogue and a vision of what really matters in these discussions. To those struggling with issues of creation and evolution, it is a godsend.

—Dr. Peter Harrison, director, Institute for Advanced Studies in the Humanities, University of Queensland

This book is not going to help you decide whether evolution is true. It does something far better! Jesus calls us to a cruciform life, and with vulnerability and candor, Wood and Falk model for us how to be Christlike in the face of serious differences that

really matter. While contemporary society knows only polarity and conflict, this book points to a countercultural way of being together in Christ.

—DR. JOHN W. HILBER, professor of Old Testament,
Grand Rapids Theological Seminary

I came to this book with much trepidation, even suspicion, and, indeed, reading it was an unsettling experience. But I also found that the stories unfolding within its pages were compelling, fascinating, and often deeply moving. And perhaps I was able also to discern the Holy Spirit of God at work in the lives of these two men, who, despite their profound, seemingly intractable differences on origins, were willing to make themselves vulnerable to engage with one another at more than a superficial level. Reading this book certainly didn't change my mind about origins, but perhaps that was never the point.

—PAUL GARNER, researcher and lecturer,
Biblical Creation Trust

I remember how often in my childhood I relished listening to a good, solid debate among my elders. The sort that looked hard into a matter, took its time to develop, and evaluated the consequences of each position. Standing at opposite ends of the current debate in evangelicalism, Todd and Darrel present us with their take on this vital and, at times, difficult debate. They do so with conviction and forcefulness coupled with humility, love, and a commitment to the Lord and his Word. The result is a serious (and very personal) dialog among respected leaders in this field. Gather round, kids. The adults are talking.

—DR. MARCUS R. ROSS, professor of geology; director,
Center for Creation Studies, Liberty University

THE
FOOL
AND THE
HERETIC

THE FOOL AND THE HERETIC

HOW TWO SCIENTISTS MOVED BEYOND LABELS TO A CHRISTIAN DIALOGUE ABOUT CREATION AND EVOLUTION

Todd Charles Wood
and Darrel R. Falk

ZONDERVAN

The Fool and the Heretic
Copyright © 2019 by Darrel R. Falk, Todd Charles Wood, and The Colossian Forum

ISBN 978-0-310-59543-4 (softcover)
ISBN 978-0-310-59546-5 (audio)
ISBN 978-0-310-59544-1 (ebook)

Requests for information should be addressed to:
Zondervan, *3900 Sparks Dr. SE, Grand Rapids, Michigan 49546*

The authors and The Colossian Forum express their deep gratitude to Lyn Cryderman for his listening ear and thoughtful engagement, which played a crucial role in helping us share our story.

Cover design: Studio Gearbox
Interior design: Denise Froehlich

Printed in the United States of America

19 20 21 22 23 /LSC/ 10 9 8 7 6 5 4 3 2 1

CONTENTS

WHAT DOES OUR FIGHTING SAY ABOUT US?

Rob Barrett, The Colossian Forum

This is the story of a disagreement. We seem to be surrounded by increasing numbers of disagreements. Today's disagreements go beyond simple differences of opinion. They're increasingly marked by breakdowns in relationships. When I learn you voted for *that* candidate, I instantly conclude there must be something wrong with you. And you think the same about me for voting for the other one. We look at each other and ask ourselves, "How could he possibly think that way?" We can't comprehend how someone could get things so wrong. And the feeling is mutual.

As we stare at each other in baffled confusion, walls

go up between us. And new walls are rising up all around us. Blacks and whites can't understand each other. It's the same with men and women, liberals and conservatives, gun owners and gun banners, mainline Christians and evangelicals, gays and straights. We try to correct the other side, but they argue or refuse to listen. We get angry, and outrage feels good (for a moment). As they continue to refuse to get it, we write them off as stupid—or evil. This sort of reactionary wall-building is the new normal. We see it every day on the news and live it out on social media and around the Thanksgiving dinner table.

Once we've written off those on the other side, we've really set ourselves up. It's only a small step from confidence in our position to self-satisfied smugness and ultimately full-blown arrogance. In anger, we call them fools, and so grant ourselves permission to belittle their intellect and then their honesty. As we dehumanize them, it becomes easy to bully them for our pleasure. My snarky jabs increase my stature among those dwelling on my side of the wall. Before long we're competing for who can create the cleverest put-downs. It escalates naturally. But it's okay because, after all, those other folks are the real arrogant bullies, not us. We start telling half-truths that favor our side, and justify them because of the huge lies the other person is telling. And they started it anyway.

Who's right and who's wrong here? The twist in

the plot comes from the way the original disagreement has receded from view. Our focus is less and less on our points of disagreement. We've shifted to a smear campaign that simply uses the issues as tools for demonstrating our superiority and their inferiority. Strangely enough, for those who have eyes to see, our differences are overshadowed by the ironic reality that our two sides find themselves strikingly agreed on how we should handle our disagreement. And it's not pretty. Whether it's Fox News or CNN, the basic teaching about how to handle our differences is the same. Bad behavior isn't the sole possession of either the left or the right.

What if there's something more important at stake than our original argument?

As Christians routinely take up this kind of all-out warfare on any number of points of disagreement (and my social media feed testifies to this reality), what does this say of us? What does it say of Jesus?

Jesus cuts through arguments in ways that bring us back to the fundamentals. His enemies tried to entrap him with the hot debate over paying taxes. But he refused the two options and challenged his followers to dig deeper to discover what it might mean to give to God what belongs to God (Matt. 22:21). What if there's something more important at stake than whether we pay taxes? When presented with a woman caught in adultery, Jesus refused to choose between judgment and mercy. Instead, he charted a reality where obedience and grace dwell together (John 7:53–8:11). What if our disagreements are about something more than who's right and who's wrong? What if our plight of division and disagreement is an opportunity for something new to appear, something worthy of Jesus? What might that look like?

We know deep in our bones that we—members of the body of Christ—belong together. It's inescapable. The apostle Paul writes, "The eye cannot say to the hand, 'I don't need you!' And the head cannot say to the feet, 'I don't need you!'" (1 Cor. 12:21). When we see members of the body of Christ walled off against each other, dividing the body into smaller and smaller silos, it pricks us. The easiest way to ward off the pain is to deny membership to the other side: Those folks can't really be Christians. Real Christians couldn't possibly think that way. Having relieved the tension with that deft move, we sigh with relief. We feel we've restored the integrity of Christ's body by amputating an arm, but it looked pretty diseased, didn't it? As new wars flare up, we run out of limbs. It dawns on us that the others have cast us off into the waste pile. Does this confirm our casting them off or suggest we've gotten something wrong? As our echo chambers shrink, and Christ's body with them, we might realize that this way of being is unsustainable.

This book is the story of a disagreement. It's a disagreement that held all of the normal promise for ugliness. It still holds that possibility. But so far, in this case, the well-worn patterns of division have given up some ground. A couple of small, amputated pieces of Christ's body have been rejoined. This happened not through anything innovative but through some meager attempts to live into the simple, and terribly difficult, patterns of childlike Christian faith. It is the story of finding a surprising—and frustrating—friend in Christ on the other side of the dividing wall.

This particular disagreement is about evolution. For some of us, the warfare between Christians over the origins of life and humanity is painfully obvious. For others, it may come as a shock to learn that there are Christians on the other side. If that's you, it's a testimony to how effective the dividing walls are. Many Christians read the early chapters of Genesis as straightforward history, with God accomplishing his creation in six days. For them, the idea of a Christian accepting evolution is as ridiculous as, well, an amoeba turning into a monkey. For Christians who long ago accepted scientific orthodoxy on any number of things, including evolution, believing in a young earth is as ridiculous as doctors bleeding patients to balance their humours. But there are many earnest Christians on both sides of that dividing wall.

If we're no longer surprised by the walls, we also shouldn't be surprised when Jesus destroys one. He has a history of doing that. Paul rejoiced at the collapse of the wall between Jews and gentiles. Jesus made something possible that was otherwise unthinkable: Jews and gentiles eating together as family. "[Christ] himself is our peace, who has made the two groups one and has destroyed the barrier, the dividing wall of hostility" (Eph. 2:14). If Jesus triumphed over this hostility with his peace, what about the hostility between Christians who accept evolution and those who reject it?

The Colossian Forum was born of the hope that Christians might do better with their conflicts. It's not just about gritting our teeth and playing nice. It's about experiencing the difference the gospel makes and showing the possibility for something new and beautiful in a world divided by conflict. Jews and gentiles eating together was a powerful display of God's wisdom (Eph. 3:10). So much effort has been put into looking for solutions to the problems at the root of our conflicts. (Does science say the earth is young or old? Is Genesis 1–3 to be read as historically precise?) But the problems remain. Worse, the war remains. Maybe it's time to try something new, or perhaps to listen anew to the ancient call of the gospel amid today's wars. Maybe we'll discover that the logs in our eyes are keeping us from seeing that the way we're engaging the war is damaging us, those we oppose, and those watching us. Jesus warned that fixating on the speck in the other's eye might reveal our own hypocrisy (Matt. 7:3–5).

The problem isn't that we disagree about things. The church has always struggled with and fought over important questions. There has never been a time when Christ's church has been pure in the sense of not being pressed by important questions where people arrive at different answers. It's exactly in such pressured disagreements that our Christlikeness (or worldliness) is most clearly revealed. While these divisive issues are important, that importance shouldn't distract us from the importance of our obedience to Christ in the *way* we engage our disagreements. What if the way we handle ourselves in our disagreements is a test of our Christian character? What if our failure to live out the gospel in the midst of these challenges is an opportunity to openly confess, repent, seek forgiveness, and try again? What if Christian disagreement provides a beautiful opportunity to proclaim not how right we are and how wrong those other people are but how good and gracious God is and how committed we want to be to putting off the old, destructive ways and putting on new, life-giving ways (Eph. 4:22–24)?

I attended an origins conference where one of the opening speakers suggested we speak humbly as we work on the divisive questions surrounding evolution.

That's a great idea! After all, Paul tells us that humility is a fundamental part of living a life worthy of Christ: "Be completely humble and gentle; be patient, bearing with one another in love" (Eph. 4:2). But isn't it a bit naive? We've tried being decent to the other side. We've learned that our efforts at gently correcting them lead nowhere. All those things we learned in children's Bible lessons are fine for children, but now we're in the big leagues and the problems are tougher. When we're tempted to set aside Jesus' teachings as foolishly simplistic, maybe warning bells should go off inside us. What if Jesus' way isn't naive but harder and more demanding than we realize? G. K. Chesterton famously wrote, "The Christian ideal has not been tried and found wanting. It has been found difficult; and left untried."[1] That conference speaker made it sound so easy to be humble and to reap the fruit that grows out of Christlike humility. It's far from easy. Living out these virtues might even be harder than understanding biology and deciding the truth or falsity of evolution. Like learning biology, learning to live like Christ takes discipline and practice. And if we're going to make any progress, we know that the real work must be done by the Holy Spirit deep in our hearts. Heaven knows we've tried and failed time and time again on our own.

As you read the story in these pages, you'll encounter two people who took up this challenge. We invited two accomplished scientists who disagree on this topic to meet each other and try to do something better, something marked by Christian love. We invited them to become friends in Christ, trusting that he had broken down their dividing wall. We were unsure how it would go, but we wanted to see whether their shared love of Jesus could make a difference even when they are so divided over an important issue. What might happen when we commit ourselves to remembering what we learned in Sunday school, even as we face grown-up challenges?

These two men are as deeply divided about the age of the earth and the theory of evolution as two people could be. As you'll read, they sincerely believe that the other one is harming the church. But they live in a single, shared world of devotion to Jesus. They know deep in their bones that they are called to love each other. Even more than this, the Holy Spirit has placed within each of them a deep desire to love each other. This love they are called to is not some fluffy, gooey thing. It is the kind of love that leads to—and through—the cross. Jesus said, "Greater love has no one than this: to lay down one's life for one's friends" (John 15:13).

Taking up a disagreement like this isn't for the faint of heart. It has not been an easy journey. In many ways we're still nearer the beginning than the end. But our two new friends have been courageous pioneers in moving out from the comfort of their camps to meet in a no-man's-land where no one knew what would happen. They have been willing to open themselves up to someone they viewed as an enemy.

After they had gotten to know and care for each other, the work stalled. We were avoiding topics when we knew the sparks might fly. To go to a level deeper, I asked them both if they truly wanted to hear the other speak honestly. One answered quickly, "Yes, I want to hear what he really thinks." The other paused and said something critically important: "Yes, I am willing for him to hurt me." Our journey together has been marked by little moments like these, when the way of Jesus has come to the surface. The world turns upside down, the loser becomes the winner, speaking truth in love isn't a contradiction, and death changes into resurrection.

Still, the challenge facing these two scientists remains. A lot is at stake, as supporters of both still want a decisive win. When will the other break down and change to join the winning team? But in God's kingdom, what does the winning team look like? To many eyes, Jesus' path looks much more like that of a loser. The way of the gospel is filled with surprises. I hope by reading these scientists' words, you will find new and surprising—perhaps even frustrating—insights into how we might learn to address our differences in ways that are worthy of Jesus.

IN THE BEGINNING

Rob Barrett, The Colossian Forum

Creation versus evolution. That was settled decades ago, right? Maybe in the 1950s or 1960s, the majority of people in the United States—and the vast majority of Christians—believed God created the heavens and the earth just as it is described in Genesis 1. But today?

It depends.

On the one hand, the Gallup organization has polled Americans on this topic more than a dozen times between 1982 and 2014, and the traditional creationist viewpoint has always been the most popular choice of those polled. The percentage of those who believe in creation has never dropped below forty percent. According to a study conducted by Jonathan Hill, a Calvin College (Michigan) professor, the issue of creation versus evolution is more nuanced, but the percentage of Americans who are absolutely or very certain that humans did not evolve from other life forms hovers around thirty percent.[1] According to the Pew Research Center, among white evangelicals, the number rejecting human evolution is much higher: sixty-four percent.[2]

In terms of the general population, then, it's safe to say that roughly thirty to forty percent of Americans believe that God created the earth pretty much as the Bible explains it in the book of Genesis. Which is kind of amazing when you consider that in the scientific community, hardly anyone believes that God created humanity apart from evolution. A 2009 poll by the Pew Research Center found that "nearly all scientists (ninety-seven percent) say humans and other living things have evolved over time."[3] And what about those Christians who are trained scientists who believe that God is somehow behind evolution? According to one source, the majority of evangelical Christian colleges teaches evolutionary creation in their science departments.[4] But those Christian professors who teach evolution remain somewhat at odds with their secular counterparts because they credit God for creating the process. The US National Academy of Sciences has stated that "creationism, intelligent design, and other claims of supernatural intervention in the origin of life or of species are not science because they are not testable by the methods of science."[5] Evolutionary creationists would agree with this critique of intelligent design, seeing it as yet another attempt to turn Christians against science.[6] For their part, nonbelieving scientists have no reason to resist the scientific contributions of their Christian colleagues. But any time a scientist brings God into the laboratory as an explanation for something, whether as a hidden hand behind evolution or orchestrating the full-blown creation of the universe several thousand years ago, alarm bells start going off. They see both of these moves as antiscience, just to different degrees.

Which brings us to our authors—Todd Charles Wood and Darrel R. Falk—two evangelical Christians with strong scientific credentials. Todd earned his PhD in biochemistry from the University of Virginia, has done postdoctoral work at Clemson University, and was on the science faculty at Bryan College. He is the founder and president of the Core Academy of Science, a research and educational organization devoted to helping Christians understand science from a young-earth creationist (YEC) point of view. Darrel's PhD in genetics is from the University of Alberta, and he did postdoctoral studies at the University of British Columbia and the University of California (Irvine). He has taught at Syracuse University, Mount Vernon Nazarene University, and Point Loma Nazarene University (where he is now professor emeritus), and is a senior advisor (and former president) of BioLogos, an organization aimed at contributing to the discussion of the relationship between science and religion from an evolutionary creation point of view. Both are really smart, really devoted to Christ, and convinced they are right about their beliefs about origins.

To the majority of scientists, Todd's views are foolish. Todd, in their view, is practicing pseudoscience. He may be really smart, but he's misleading others by misusing his intelligence. Ironically, to many YECs, he's a traitor because he sometimes questions the science of his fellow creationists. Darrel, on the other hand, is only slightly less foolish than Todd. He is an evangelical Christian, after all, and fewer than six percent of leading biologists believe in a personal God who hears and answers prayers—a central tenet of evangelical Christianity and a foundation stone of Darrel's faith and life.[7] To many Christians, however, Darrel is a false teacher because he does not believe the earth was created the way Genesis 1 seems to them to describe it. Well-known evangelical leader John MacArthur has referred to what Darrel is doing as a "heinous crime" that is "destroying people's confidence in Scripture."[8] To such Christians, if you accept evolutionary creation, you are a heretic.

The evangelical Christian community isn't real sure what to do with Todd and Darrel. Only twenty-seven percent of white, evangelical Protestants accept the theory of evolution.[9] And yet, despite Todd's credentials, he likely would not be hired to teach science at the majority of Christian colleges, at least not classic evangelical institutions such as Wheaton, Calvin, Taylor, Seattle Pacific, Gordon, Westmont, and Asbury. Bryan College, his employer for thirteen years, is one of only a handful of Christian liberal arts colleges and universities that teach young-earth creationism within their science departments. And while Darrel is beloved by his Christian college colleagues, when he began his career (initially in secular universities) with his evolutionary creation perspective, he was quite certain that there would be no room for him in evangelical churches. Having grown up in one such church, he longed to be a part but didn't expect there would be room for him and his family. He heard his perspective repeatedly mocked on Christian radio and felt that his view was considered not only wrong but just plain sinful.

Thus, we have Dr. Todd Charles Wood, a fool, and Dr. Darrel R. Falk, a heretic. Except that both love Jesus and neither is foolish. If you're part of the majority of evangelical Christians who believe God created the earth in six days a few thousand years ago, what do you do with Darrel? Would you send your daughter to his Christian college, spending more than thirty thousand dollars a year for her to be taught that God created over a long period of time instead of in six days a relatively short time ago? Would you invite him to attend your small group at church or to teach a Sunday school class about other aspects of Christian living, given that he works with Scripture on matters of faith and practice in ways strikingly similar to Todd's?

And if you are among those in the church who think that evolution is the tool God has used to carry out his creation command, what would you do with Todd? Would you respect him as a scientist? Would you invite him to teach why he holds the view he does despite the fact that he admits that the overwhelming scientific evidence seems to be to the contrary?

A basic human question that interests me is what would Darrel and Todd do with each other? What would happen if I got them in the same room? Would they get along with each other? Could they worship together? Pray together? Love each other? For the most part, Christians who accept the theory of evolution have essentially ignored their fellow believers who are young-earth creationists. Or worse. Many in the evolution community have said very unkind things about the intellect and motivation of young-earth creationists. Darrel himself has raised the question of whether what Todd is doing is consistent with the standards of true scientific inquiry. Creationists, on the other hand, have become increasingly vocal—and harsh—in their criticism of evolutionary creationists. As I mentioned, popular author and preacher John MacArthur described what Darrel is doing as a "heinous crime" that is "destroying people's confidence in Scripture."[10] Ken Ham, founder of the creationist organization Answers in Genesis, writes that the way Christian evolutionists like Darrel interpret Genesis is "nothing more than fallible sinful man's attempts not to take God at His Word."[11] Todd would not go that far, but he does not think what Darrel is doing is benign.

In 2013, I invited Todd and Darrel to meet with me and a few of my colleagues who have a keen interest in how Christians address their differences. It's one of many projects my organization, The Colossian Forum, sponsors to learn how Christians who vehemently disagree on serious issues can address them in a way that honors Christ and each other. Few topics generate as much heat among conservative Christians as creation versus evolution, and both men are unwavering in their views. That they have developed a deep, caring friendship over these years is a testament to Christ's work in what would be a disharmonious relationship. That is not to say it has been easy. Our first meeting was difficult, especially for Todd, who was concerned that he would be belittled. And he was at one point, by Darrel, who recognized he needed to apologize for incorrectly stating that Todd was not well informed about evolutionary theory. Just prior to the apology, the tension was rife, and I wasn't sure there would be a second meeting. As you will read, the issues surrounding their disagreement reach to the core of our Christian faith and witness. It's not just that each thinks the other is wrong about how the earth began. In a way, that's the easy part. If that were all that is at stake, they could agree to disagree, wish each other well, and go their separate ways. But there's much, much more at stake.

And that's as good a place as any to begin.

———— For Study and Reflection ————

1. What is your belief about how the earth and all that is in it began?
2. What has most influenced your thinking on this topic?
3. How would your family and friends respond if you changed your views on this topic?
4. How would you respond to the following point of view, which some Christians have: "It really doesn't matter what you believe about origins just as long as you believe in God and accept his free gift of salvation"?
5. Does your church hold to a specific view of origins, and if so, how is that communicated or taught to children? Teenagers? Adults?

6. How do you think your pastor or small group leader would respond if you asked them to invite someone to speak who disagrees with your church's teaching on creation?

CHAPTER 1

WHY DARREL IS WRONG
AND WHY IT MATTERS

Todd Charles Wood

Darrel R. Falk is right about a lot of things. He's right when he says that evolutionary scientists have collected a vast amount of evidence supporting the theory of evolution. He's right when he says that there's evidence supporting the evolution of humans from animals over millions of years. He's right when he says that evolution is an extremely successful theory, accepted almost without question by a huge majority of the world's scientists.

But all of that evidence and all of that support don't make evolution true. The grand story of evolution from the first primitive cells to our modern world teeming with living things is false, which means Darrel and any other scientist who believes that evolution accurately describes how this world of living things developed are mistaken.

I am not surprised that a non-Christian scientist would accept the theory of evolution, nor am I all that surprised that Christians like Darrel might see no conflict between their faith in Christ and acceptance of evolution. But I am deeply troubled by Christians who promote the compatibility of Christianity and evolution. Ultimately, I believe they are dangerous. I believe that Darrel and other Christian evolutionists are harming the church.

Christians who accept evolution inevitably must modify their understanding of Genesis 1–11, which sparks one theological crisis after another. In essence, they read Genesis and say, "Well, it doesn't really mean what it says." Some might reason that the days of creation actually represent a long time, perhaps millions or even billions of years. Others would claim that Genesis is not intended to give us an exact description of how and when God created the heavens and the earth. Instead, it's written in the tradition of the creation myth, a kind of theology written in narrative form, like the parables of Jesus. The details are unimportant, they say; it's only the theological message that matters.

I find Darrel's approach to Scripture profoundly unconvincing. I cannot find the logical consistency in this effort to bend Scripture to fit their science. It seems to me that there's an arbitrary decision that in this particular part of God's Word, he doesn't really mean what he says. In other parts, well, of course he does. He means exactly what he says. But in Genesis, not so much. Why? Well, it's obviously inconvenient from the perspective of science.

As Darrel and his colleagues attempt to "reimagine" what already seems pretty clear to me in Genesis, I see other passages that require "reimagining" too. For example, is Exodus 20:11 wrong when it declares, "For in six days the LORD made the heavens and the earth, the sea, and all that is in them"? What about the apostle Paul and his detailed discussion of Adam's sin in his epistles to the Corinthians and Romans? (To be fair to Darrel, I know that he and many evolutionary creation advocates accept the possibility of a historical Adam, but some don't.) Or what about Peter's discussion of the end times and the flood? If these passages which seem so clear don't really mean what they say, how in the world can we know that any part of the Bible means what it says?

Even more troubling is the possibility of errors in God's Word. Some of Darrel's colleagues would have us believe that the Bible endorses false ideas about history or the creation because those details were not important. Most won't come out and say that the Bible is wrong, but that's certainly what's implied. With these theological machinations, Darrel and his colleagues raise hard questions about the authority and trustworthiness of the Bible, and once that happens, a lot of things will need to change for evangelicals. Once you disavow this very clear and important part of the Bible, what's stopping us from disavowing other parts of the Bible that also are difficult to explain scientifically, like the resurrection? It's not just a slippery slope but an inevitability when you start pulling out the threads from the fabric of our faith. That's exactly what Darrel wants to do. He's confident he's just pulling on a few loose threads, but I think once you start pulling, as he has done, the whole fabric of theology will unravel.

Here's an example of how Christian evolutionists fiddle with the faith to make evolution compatible. Darrel and some of his colleagues like to point out that science has nothing to say about a historical Adam and Eve, but scientists tell us that modern humans evolved from a population of thousands of individuals. So how does that fit with the Bible's depiction of Adam and Eve? Darrel and company contend that there were indeed other humans on the earth, but that Adam and Eve were singled out by God for a special purpose. There's nothing in science to stop them from believing this, and it makes it easier to talk about Paul's teaching on Adam if there really was an Adam. To them, this is a "safe" way to harmonize science and the Bible, but what they have done is completely alter the reality of who Adam and Eve were according to God's

Word. Eve is no longer the mother of all living (Gen. 3:20), and human nations are no longer made from one (Acts 17:26). An Edenic Adam as "tribal chief" is not the Adam of the Bible.

Darrel himself has acknowledged that this is exactly what happened in the mainline denominations. They went all-in on "higher criticism," and where are they now? Even the most generous observers of mainline churches would agree that they have been in decline for decades, and I believe a big part of the cause of that decline is their zeal to make the Bible say what they want it to say. They want to recreate God in their own image. As I watch people stumbling down that slope to apostasy, I can't understand why Darrel and other Christian evolutionists aren't concerned that they might be headed in the same direction. To be fair, I think Darrel understands what's at stake and is pretty stubborn about where he applies this type of interpretation to Scripture. That's reassuring, but it seems so arbitrary. How do he and his colleagues decide when the Bible means what it says and when it doesn't? Is the measuring rod really going to be what science or culture tells us is true about science or history? Do we stop reinterpreting only because we're stubborn and don't want to give up miracles or the resurrection? We can't really expect personal stubbornness to make a good foundation for theology.

After all, if really clear science is the reason we have to reimagine two thousand years of theology, why stop with evolution? We have just as much scientific evidence that says when you're dead, you're dead. Yet in the New Testament, we read that Jesus was killed by the cruel method of crucifixion, that he was clearly dead when his followers took him off the cross and carried him to his tomb. Three days later, the tomb was empty. This victory over death—a scientific impossibility—is the fundamental cornerstone of our Christian faith. When I mention this scientific inconsistency in the Bible to Darrel and other Christian evolutionists, they just shrug and say, "Well, the resurrection is a miracle." Of course it is! And so is creation! Why accept one miracle in the Bible and reject another, unless, of course, you are allowing science to influence your theology? And what's keeping you from one day looking at the evidence and deciding that, you know what, science tells us that death is final. It's medically impossible to revive a person who has been dead for three days. The resurrection must not have really happened as it is described in the Bible. Plenty of former Christians have made this move. Why not Christian evolutionists? Once again, to be fair, I know that Darrel fully believes in the resurrection, even though scientifically it doesn't make any sense at all.

I have a hard time avoiding the conclusion that our

standing with the world is a big motivation for Christian evolutionists. They want to be accepted by the broader scientific community. Darrel has said as much when he has expressed his concern that if he held to the creation account, he would lose any opportunity to influence secular scientists with his Christian faith. I can appreciate his evangelistic spirit, but I haven't seen any evidence that mainstream scientists are becoming Christians in droves because Darrel and others accept the theory of evolution. And even if Darrel can show a few testimonies of people coming to faith through the ministry of Christian evolutionists, I can show many more testimonies of people coming to faith through the ministry of young-age creationists.[1]

The unpleasant reality is that evolution itself is dangerous. It is not unusual for young people who have been taught creation in their churches to go off to a Christian college, become influenced by evolution, and ultimately abandon their faith. Unfortunately, I've seen the same thing happen with students who left the Christian college where I used to teach. They went to a secular university to pursue a postgraduate degree, accepted evolution, and left the faith.

If this fad of Christian evolution prevails—if we continue to interpret Scripture to accommodate the prevailing culture—we will lose our Christian identity. We will become a dead, irrelevant nonchurch, like every other church that has tried to make peace with the "wisdom" of the world. It might not happen in Darrel's personal life, but it will happen. We will also lose an amazingly fruitful and exciting avenue of scientific research that goes deeper than Darwin, and that would be a shame. And we would certainly lose an enormous amount of time, people, and resources to something that simply isn't true.

I have not yet discovered satisfying answers to every question raised by the theory of evolution. Because I believe the Bible means what it says, I trust that the answers are out there. That trust in the Bible might have alienated me from other mainstream scientists, but followers of Christ were never called to be like everyone else. How much more could be accomplished for both science and the kingdom if Darrel and all the other gifted scientists who love Jesus joined me in using our knowledge to explore the incredibly beautiful mysteries of God's creation just as he described it in Genesis!

For Study and Reflection

1. How would you respond to a person who accepts much of the evidence proving the earth is round, yet still believes it is flat? Would you admire their commitment? Criticize them for their stubbornness? Dismiss them as irrelevant? Why?

2. Todd says that followers of Christ should not be like everyone else. In what ways has your faith influenced you to be unlike everyone else? In what ways do you think some Christians try too hard to be like everyone else?

3. Should Christians care whether science supports their beliefs in supernatural events such as the virgin birth or the resurrection? Why or why not?

4. Most young-earth creationists are critical of Todd for acknowledging that evolutionists have collected a large volume of credible evidence. What do you think? Is he hurting the cause by giving evolutionists so much credit? Or is he giving creationists greater credibility?

5. Todd believes that evolutionary Christians like Darrel are contributing to the church's becoming dead or irrelevant. Do you agree? Why or why not?

6. Can you think of other examples where the ways Christians believe are hurting the church? How would you respond to a fellow Christian who you think is causing harm to the church?

CHAPTER 2

WHY TODD IS WRONG AND
WHY IT MATTERS

Darrel R. Falk

Todd Charles Wood is somewhat of an anomaly to me. Over the years, I have known and interacted with many scientists or science educators who hold a young-earth perspective. I have learned much about faith from them. I have appreciated their sincerity, their deep love for the Lord, and their earnestness for the kingdom of God. Our conversations have not always been easy. Most of them believe that mainstream science has many weaknesses and that evolutionary theory is about to fail. Some are deeply concerned about the work in which I am engaged, considering me to be an agent of Satan. Amazingly, though, they have all been nice to me, and

I enjoy being with them. Almost always I have sensed that Christ is at work in their lives. Jesus is clearly able to work through them despite what I think is their ignorance about how science works and especially about the overwhelming nature of the evidence for God's working through the evolutionary process.

Todd is just like them in the depth and beauty of his faith. He is following Jesus, and I love to be there alongside of him whenever we are together. What is different about Todd is that his PhD is in molecular evolution. He hasn't come into creation science from some side-biological discipline like medicine, cell biology, microbiology, or physiology. Todd's graduate training is in evolution itself. In that regard, he is somewhat like another young-earth creationist I've had the privilege of meeting, Kurt Wise, who has a Harvard PhD in paleontology with one of the twentieth century's most influential evolutionary biologists, Stephen Jay Gould. Todd, like Kurt, knows and acknowledges just how strong the scientific case is for evolution. Both of them know the science so well, and both of them are individuals of such high integrity, that they are constitutionally incapable of distorting the science even though it doesn't fit their views. Todd, like Kurt, is the first to admit that evolution is not a theory in crisis. He is quite certain that it is wrong, but he thinks that most of the arguments put forward by people who come at the question without graduate training in evolutionary biology are scientifically naive and poorly constructed. Todd, like Kurt and a small group of others, thinks that the best way of showing that evolutionary biology is wrong is to develop the creation model in a manner that puts forward testable hypotheses. Theirs is a positive agenda, rather than a defensive attack on the science of evolution. If Scripture is the Word of God, Todd believes, then posing the right scientific questions and studying them will eventually show why evolutionary biology is wrong and a literalistic interpretation of Genesis is correct. I appreciate his willingness to objectively look at the evidence for evolution rather than to simply dismiss it or ridicule those of us who accept it.

Finally, Todd's awfully nice, and I've grown to appreciate his efforts not only to get to know me better—few young-earth creationists have done that—but to treat me with the utmost respect and kindness. I also appreciate that Todd repeatedly reminds me of Jesus. Not only is he very gentle and kind, but he gets excited, really excited, about creation. Sometimes when I'm with Todd, I feel a little of the excitement that I think is the driving force behind creation itself. God loves all of creation more than we can imagine. He designed it and he delights in it. When I'm with Todd and he gets going on the thrill of being a biologist, I feel a bit like I'm with Jesus and feel a bit of the excitement he, as the Creator of it all, must feel when he examines the beauty of life's processes. Todd has that same kind of joy, and as a scientist who also celebrates all that Christ has made, I find it fun to be around him. He is effervescent with joy, even during those times when I awkwardly express my thoughts about whether his project is going to be fruitful.

As a scientist, what I respect most about Todd is that he's not out to disprove or discredit the theory of evolution. Rather, he has devoted his professional life to building a scientific case for young-earth creationism. In a textbook he recently wrote for students in Christian schools or those being homeschooled, he acknowledges that humans and apes are similar but encourages students to use science to find out *why* they are similar. In other words, "Don't fight the evidence of evolution; dig deeper into science for a better answer." That's a refreshingly different approach to young-earth creationism. Todd believes that one day in the future, the creation science he is doing will finally add up, convincing me and my fellow evolutionary creationists that the earth was created in six days a relatively short time ago. It would be great if other young-earth creationists and the organizations they belong to would become as well informed by getting graduate degrees in evolutionary biology like Todd has done and then developing positive and rigorous scientific tests for predictions of the creation model. To that end, I support what Todd is doing. He brings a much-needed scientific seriousness to the table, and he is open to honest dialogue and debate, always treating those who disagree with him with respect, even kindness.

While I genuinely admire Todd's passion for finding scientific evidence for creation—I really do—he will fail because he is just plain wrong. He knows that I think he will fail because the evidence for evolution is vastly overwhelming. Although I know it will never happen, sometimes I wish Todd would stop and join forces with me in a joint endeavor. I think we are really very close in our views of Scripture, so it wouldn't take much of a shift in Todd's position for him to come over to my scientific view—a shift in how he interprets only a few chapters. I think there is figurative language in the Genesis account and he doesn't. Other than that (and a few other issues in Genesis 1–11), we look at Scripture and the Christian life in almost the same way. His background is Baptist and mine is Wesleyan/Holiness, so there are a few denominational differences, but man, it sure seems to me we're almost on the same page. Unlike some evangelical evolutionary Christians, I am even comfortable with a historical Adam and Eve (see John Walton's *Lost World of Adam and Eve*), so we're oh so close on the Bible, but oh so far apart on science.

It's not just that Todd is wrong, but I believe he is harming the church by promoting his view of origins, and it pains me to say that. Todd is a good man, a brother in Christ, and I do not like thinking that such a person is causing harm to the church, but I can't help the fact that I do. The more the church embraces the view of creation that he accepts, the less influence it will have on those who need to experience the beautiful gift of the abundant life offered by Jesus.

Scientists in general—and certainly the leading figures in biology today—have pretty much concluded that there's no need anymore for any kind of religion. It's an artifact of our past. Most scientists would say that the era of belief in God is behind us and that we have to move on. That concerns me for at least two reasons. First, most of the laws and values in our culture have been shaped by a Judeo-Christian heritage. People who have attempted to live by the teachings of Scripture have had a positive influence on our culture. Increasingly, we are seeing that influence wane. I would hate to think what our culture would be like if we lost that influence.

The overarching reason why I worry about the increasing secularization of our culture, however, is that I believe that the only hope for the world is Christ in the lives of believers. This is not the place to elaborate on the huge world crises that may be on the horizon as we move deeper into a technology-driven society, but if ever there has been a need for Christ's presence (which is manifest through us), it is now. If Christians are off in a corner basically talking to themselves and not speaking into this culture that has been so influenced recently by a secular scientism, then we are not carrying out our task of witnessing effectively by offering what the apostle Paul describes as "the hope of glory" to the rest of the world.

Every time Todd and other young-earth creationists convince a Christian that the earth was created in six days less than ten thousand years ago, they are contributing to the declining influence of the Christian faith on culture, as well as to the prevailing view among scientists and many in our culture that Christianity is a relic that holds no interest for them. The world desperately needs the gospel; Christians need to be speaking into that world. But they will not be taken seriously if they continue to believe that the earth is ten thousand years old, and a significant portion of them do.

The more the church rallies around the young-earth flag, the greater opportunity we give to scientism to prevail, and that would be disastrous for our culture. As much as I've come to admire Todd and respect him as a scientist, I believe Christians who embrace and promote young-earth creationism are contributing to the dismissal of Christianity within the scientific and academic communities, and because those institutions wield so much influence over all of culture, it is not an overstatement to say that the young-earth creationist movement presents a barrier to the gospel to many.

It's easy for me to see why today's scientific community dismisses not only Todd's work but his faith as well. Those who even bother to look into what he is doing would likely say that he's not really doing science, and I would tend to agree. Remember, I do not question Todd's scientific credentials. They are impeccable. What he does is really logical in that he uses the techniques of science, makes hypotheses as any good scientist would, and conducts research to try to find support for those hypotheses. It really looks like science. But I have a real problem with the way Todd almost capriciously dismisses the volumes of evidence for evolution. If you ignore the overwhelming amount of evidence coming in for a theory from all different corners and disciplines, all of which point in the same direction and are fully and totally consistent with each other—if you ignore this overwhelming body of evidence, I'm not sure that what you're doing is science anymore. It may be interesting, but it's not science.

I understand why Todd cannot bring himself to accept and trust the voluminous body of evidence for evolution. He believes all of the Bible is literalistically true, and he is trying to use the tools of science to support that belief.

But at some point you have to abandon science to do that, and it appears that he has done just that. He has chosen a literalistic interpretation of the Bible over the indisputable evidence from science, and that's why scientists can so easily dismiss not only his science but also his faith. Any scientist (and members of society at large who are so influenced by science) who is not a Christian and is presented with the young-earth creationist point of view will almost certainly say, "If that's what I must believe in order to be a Christian, I cannot become a Christian." To be fair, Todd does not insist that you have to be a young-earth creationist in order to be a Christian. But in the broader scientific community, creationism is almost always associated with Christianity, which in practice means if you reject creationism, you are basically rejecting Christianity, which is what the majority of scientists have done. And to me, that's very sad and unnecessary.

Russell Stannard, a professor of physics at the Open University in the United Kingdom and a Christian who accepts evolution, once observed, "Literalist, fundamentalist Christians have always bothered me. On the one hand, they clearly have a deep respect and love for the Bible, which I unreservedly applaud. But theirs is an approach that appears to fly in the face of the scientific evidence. . . . The creationist movement remains powerful, especially in the USA. Sadly, its activities lead to a significant number of scientists becoming contemptuous of all religion."[1]

Todd's belief in creationism not only is creating a barrier for unbelievers but also is driving many Christian young people away from the faith. This hits close to home for me, as I will explain later, but I have seen what happens when a person is taught in his or her church that God created the earth in six days, and then is confronted with the convincing evidence of evolution. Many conclude that if they have been misled about this biblical "fact," then perhaps the whole Christian story is also a lie. I believe truth always points to God. There are few things about which I am more certain than I am about evolution. It is the process that God has used and continues to use to create all of life on earth. On the other hand, that which is untrue ultimately leads humanity away from God. I know Todd means well and clearly disagrees with me, but ultimately, the truth of evolution is supported by too much evidence to be disputed. In the meantime, his efforts to convince others of something that is not true is harming the church and her witness.

We're heading deeper and deeper into a scientific age where we will be confronted with huge issues relating to the brain, neuroscience, and other ethical minefields. For example, genetic enhancement is no longer science fiction. The biological engineering of human beings could be used in ways that are both helpful and harmful, which is why scientists who follow Jesus need a voice when it comes to ethical questions surrounding this field of science. Our understanding of human nature is vastly different from that of most in the scientific community, who think that humans are not created in the image of almighty God but are the accidental products of a godless 3.5-billion-year-old impersonal algorithm called natural selection. We need to encourage young people to become scientists of the highest order so that the Christian message is present and respected in that environment. If they embrace the young-earth creationist perspective, they will not have a place at the table. They will remain in their silos and therefore have no influence on what is happening in the greater scientific world. And if they are taught by the church that they must accept creationism in order to remain Christians, they will eventually, perhaps even reluctantly, leave the faith. Already, the leading biological scientists are largely atheistic, and the discipline will only separate itself farther from Christianity if we tell our young people they have to believe in a young, recently created earth.

Yes, Todd is both a deeply committed Christian and a well-trained scientist. I know he believes he is on a quest that will ultimately find scientific support for a literal interpretation of Genesis 1, and there is certainly something admirable about that. But even though his honest, science-based approach separates him from the work of other young-earth creationists, it is having the same effect, which is bringing harm to the church.

────── For Study and Reflection ──────

1. Many if not most young-earth creationists believe the work that Darrel and other evolutionary Christians are doing is "the work of Satan." Is this a fair criticism? Why or why not?

2. How could holding a young-earth creationist view be a deterrent to evangelism?

3. Darrel believes that to accept a literalistic interpretation of Genesis 1, you have to abandon science. How would you describe your own views of science and the Bible? If science seems to contradict the Bible, what do you do?

4. Can you think of other areas where the church needs to change its views in order to become a more effective witness to the world? Explain.

5. What advice would you give to a young person who wants to pursue a career in science and holds a young-earth creationist point of view?

6. To what extent should pastors attempt to influence their congregations on the topic of origins? Explain.

CARING ENOUGH TO CONFRONT

Rob Barrett, The Colossian Forum

That was not easy for Todd and Darrel. They were unable to confront each other in this manner when they first started meeting to discuss their views of origins. Generally, Christians choose one of two options when they disagree sharply over something that is important to them and that they believe is critical to their faith. Some draw a circle tighter, pushing out those who do not agree with them. Often, those within and outside the circle then become contentious, even mean toward each other. Obviously, this approach does not honor Christ, who by his word and example calls us to love our enemies.

Others enter a tacit agreement that they will not address the subject over which they disagree. Whenever an issue comes up where we know there will be differences, we become afraid that addressing it will destroy us, destroy relationships, destroy the church. Nobody wants any part of that, so we avoid talking about it. We block out the issue as if it weren't there. While this is a pragmatic alternative to the "divide and criticize" approach, it creates a false sense of community that violates our Lord's new command that we love one another.

Neither Todd nor Darrel is capable of the first option and have too much integrity to pretend their disagreement doesn't exist. But it wasn't until they grew in their relationship with each other and got to know each other that they were able to say to each other, "You are wrong, and your wrongness is pretty serious." Yet even then, these were difficult conversations.

Understanding another person requires more than knowing what they think and why. Our thinking is connected to our story of how we got there. Darrel and Todd listened carefully to each other's stories. They—and I—find it interesting how both grew up in loving Christian families, faithfully attended small conservative evangelical churches, shared a deep interest in science, yet came to such different conclusions about how the earth came into existence. Fascinating stories worth sharing.

CHAPTER 3

BEAUTIFUL WORLD, BEAUTIFUL SAVIOR

Todd Charles Wood

I don't know where I got my passion for science, exploration, and discovery. Sometimes people can recall epiphanies they had when they were kids. Suddenly the sky parted, the angels began singing, and their divine calling descended from heaven. Nothing like that happened to me. I just always liked science.

Maybe you could blame my grandfather.

One of my earliest memories of science happened when I was about seven or eight years old. My grandpa pulled into our driveway with a huge pile of old books in the back of his truck. I have no idea where he got them. Maybe it was an estate sale. All I remember is that I spied a dusty old anatomy textbook and claimed it for my own. It was an old copy of Logan Clendening's *The Human Body*. The writing was way above my head at that age, but the diagrams were not. I remember poring over that book so much that I eventually memorized the names of the major bones in the body. All before I hit fifth grade.

Thus began my strange obsession with bones.

I was blessed to grow up in the rural Midwest—in farm country, surrounded by fields and trees, creeks and swamps. When other kids took to the ball field after school, I trekked through a virtual biology lab outside my house, always on the lookout for, well—bones. I started a little collection after discovering some cat skulls from the local population of barn cats. My collection grew as I discovered deer bones and even a pig skull. Mom wouldn't let me keep those "dirty things" in the house, of course, so they had to be stored outside in one of our sheds.

To me, these bones weren't filthy. They were fascinating and beautiful pieces of the animal kingdom that satisfied a boy's curiosity about how things work. Intricate parts that fit perfectly together allowing that animal—in its better days—to run or hop or slither off in search of food or shelter. It may have seemed odd to others, this child fascinated by bones. It may seem odd to you. But there was nothing odd about it to me.

I still have many of those bones, and I keep them in

my office now. There's a beautiful cat skull, a ragged old horse skull, and some others that I added later in life. None of them are worth much as scientific specimens, but they're worth a lot to me. They remind me of my childhood and how deeply ingrained my love for science really is.

About the same time that I started reading *The Human Body*, I began taking my role as a budding scientist quite seriously, posting a paper sign on my bedroom door: "Dr. Todd Charles Wood." My parents, perhaps understanding that there were worse things I could be obsessed with, supported my scientific aspirations. On the occasion of my tenth Christmas, they replaced that paper sign with a plastic nameplate they had professionally made for me. They got me an even nicer one years later, when my doctorate was official, but I still like that little plastic one.

As I said, I don't really know for sure where my passion for science came from, but I do recall something else that helped prepare me to become a scientist: high school English classes. I know that doesn't make a whole lot of sense, but I learned some really important skills from my high school teachers. I vividly remember that our class spent an entire semester working on research papers. Most of my friends hated it, but I really got into the whole idea of going to the library—the big downtown one that had the most books and magazines—and researching a topic, taking notes from my research, and then writing a narrative about it. I went way overboard with old references I got from the basement archives, but I was hooked. Chasing down information and following trails of references was oddly addicting. That year, I started keeping files full of photocopied articles about subjects that interested me. I was fifteen.

In an English literature class, I began to learn how to think carefully and critically. You might remember from your literature classes that we could never just read a story and move on. Teachers always had to assign questions about what we'd read. Those questions inevitably asked about the symbolism or meaning of the story, and I had trouble making sense of them, especially if I didn't particularly like the story. But in Mr. Barsuhn's literature class, the lightbulb finally came on, and I began to understand how to answer those questions. I started to see the symbolism for myself, without being told what it was. I began to interpret what I read. All those skills my teachers had been trying to teach me over the years finally crystallized in one fall semester. I could *think*.

Even though I'd always wanted to be a scientist, I had no idea how that works—how you actually go from being a weird kid who collects bones to being a bona fide practicing scientist. As I thought about college at the end of my high school years, I decided the best way to become a scientist was to get my bachelor's degree and work as a science teacher for a few years while I saved money to pay for graduate school. I didn't really know any scientists, and I didn't really understand how to get a career in science. But I knew I wanted to pursue science as a creationist, because I was a Christian.

Faith for me was about as natural as breathing. My parents were charter members of the Baptist church I attended. At five years old, I committed my life to Christ, and at no time did I ever have any doubts about how the world and everything in it came into being. God created it. That's what the Bible said. That's what my church taught me. I never saw reason to question it. I know that a lot of Christian young people have big existential crises about their faith, especially today, but I never did. I just knew that God was real and that I belonged to him.

When it came time for college, my parents wanted me to go to a Christian college for two years, but I thought, why not all four years? So off I went to Liberty University, where I began to grow as a "real" scientist and, at the same time, learned that there were a lot of other serious scientists who believed in creation. As a kid, my only exposure to creationism was a copy of *The Genesis Flood* that belonged to my parents and a tiny little paperback with the audacious title *The Handy Dandy Evolution Refuter*. I had never seen a scholarly journal, so when I discovered the journal room in Liberty's library, it was like I had died and gone to heaven. This was a real library, and journals were so much better than magazines or newspapers! That room was where I first discovered the Creation Research Society. I never knew such a thing existed. That's how I entered the larger world of young-age creationism.

Ironically, Liberty was also where I began to think very carefully about some things that creationists believed. I had a few intellectual crises, very much like any student raised in a Christian home. I call them crises, but that may be giving them more importance than they probably deserve. A better word might be puzzles. The first puzzle had to do with dinosaur nests and how they were formed. I remember reading John Horner's *Digging Dinosaurs* and discovering that dinosaur nests were found in multiple layers in the same location. I wasn't sure how that could happen during a global flood. One layer of nests being buried by the flood made sense to me, but how could dinosaurs come back *during* the flood and make more nests? That didn't make sense to me.

The other puzzle arose when I tried to write a research paper on the "vapor canopy theory," an old creationist idea about the world before the flood. I remember being discouraged by the lack of resources on the subject. I had heard about the canopy, and I knew a lot about what it supposedly did before the flood. But I could find very little in the library about it. Another student in my position might have switched topics, but I was stubborn and turned in a lousy paper. I got a C.[1]

Unlike so many other students who hit this sort of crisis and slid down that slippery slope, I never really doubted my faith or my belief in creationism. It never occurred to me that what is described in Genesis could be wrong. Instead, I thought that my understanding of the flood was just naive and that an answer to the dinosaur nest puzzle would eventually be found. The canopy mess helped me understand that some parts of creationism persisted as folklore rather than as documented research. I became convinced that creationists just needed to be better scientists and scholars. We needed to work toward a better understanding of God's creation, and we needed to properly document our work.

After receiving my degree from Liberty, I skipped the career as a science teacher altogether. Much to my surprise, my professors at Liberty told me about these things called fellowships that let you go straight to graduate school in science for free. Even though it seemed too good to be true, I applied, and just a month after finishing at Liberty, I began a doctoral program at the University of Virginia to study evolutionary biochemistry. I worked alongside some excellent scientists, many of whom raised their eyebrows when they learned I'd done my undergraduate work at Liberty. Graduate school was a huge challenge to my thinking, and what I learned stretched me far beyond what I understood as a little fifth-grade bone collector.

I remember in my first semester sitting in class listening to a lecture on protein evolution that really rocked my world. (I'm going to get technical for a bit here, so if you skim the next couple of paragraphs and don't exactly understand what I'm talking about, that's okay.) I already knew that proteins are strings of twenty different chemicals called amino acids, and that the order or sequence of the amino acids is what determines the protein's function. What do proteins do? Almost everything. If there's a chemical reaction that happens in your body (like digesting food, muscle contraction, or thinking), there's one or more proteins controlling it.

As I listened to this lesson on protein evolution, the professor explained that you could take corresponding proteins from different species and compare their sequences. For example, mice have a protein called hemoglobin made of four sequences of amino acids. If you compared those sequences to the hemoglobin taken from a rat, they would be surprisingly similar, but not identical. At that point, I wasn't surprised, since rats and mice are both mammals and I would expect them to have similar proteins.

The professor went on to explain that you could

tabulate the differences found in pairs of similar proteins. For example, in hemoglobin, you might find that the mouse has an amino acid called serine at one spot, and the rat has a threonine at the very same spot. If you tallied all the differences from pairs of similar proteins, you would find that the differences aren't random. You could even calculate an evolutionary chart—a completely manufactured chart, mind you—showing how similar amino acids are based on how they match up in sequences that are nearly identical. With that chart, called a PAM matrix, you could turn around and identify protein similarity between humans and bacteria.[2]

I remember thinking, "Wow! That's a great argument for evolution, and I don't know how to answer it." I had always just fallen back on the idea that creatures are similar because God (a common designer) made them that way. Designers always have common features in their different works, right? As I sat in that protein evolution lecture, I realized that the similarity of organisms is far more sophisticated and intricate than I'd ever suspected. By observing similarities between proteins, you could predict the sorts of ways that proteins would be similar. This went way beyond *The Handy Dandy Evolution Refuter*.

As I learned more about evolution, I found that much of what I knew about creationism didn't fully explain the evidence. At best, young-age creationism had provided a skeleton upon which explanations might be built. At worst, some of the creationist claims I had heard were just wrong. If someone at the time had demanded I give a creationist explanation of the PAM matrix, I couldn't have done it.

Once again, those challenges did not discourage me. They still don't. My faith in God and in his Word is still unshaken, and I still love science because it is the best way to explore God's creation. Science is how we try to understand the natural world. Even though the Bible tells us the absolute truth about creation, the Bible gives us very little detail about the natural world. If you want to understand those details, if you want to know what proteins look like, you need to use science.

What does that mean for the PAM matrix? After twenty years of pondering that subject, I think the evolutionary argument is just upside down. In class I learned that tracking amino acid substitutions in the short term determines what sort of substitutions can be tolerated over billions of years of evolutionary time. But what if the answer is the other way around? What if the design principles God used to create protein diversity in the first place determine what sort of amino acid substitutions are tolerated in the short term? That doesn't explain everything about protein similarity, but it makes sense. It's a place to start.

As a creationist, I'm very confident that I understand the outline of history that God revealed in Genesis. If the creation account is true—if the earth was formed a few thousand years ago, if there was a global flood—then we should be able to use those ideas to interpret what we see in the natural world, and ultimately creation science should work better than any evolutionary science. I just need to figure out the details of how Genesis history relates to the evidence left behind in creation, and to do that I use science. That's exciting to me because I'm able to use what God has given to me to understand his creation. I can look back on my life now and see how God has drawn me into this wonderful quest for understanding his creation and ultimately the Creator himself. The more I study, the greater amazement I have for God and the world that he created!

For Study and Reflection

1. Todd grew up in a small, rural community, attended a small, conservative church, and never seriously questioned what he had been taught about origins. What's your story? How did you come to believe what you do about origins?
2. Have you changed your mind about something important to you? If so, what factors influenced that change?

If not, why do you think you've been able to avoid challenges to your thinking?

3. Darrel has said that many young people who hold to a young-earth creationist view abandon their faith or at least go through some serious questioning once they are introduced to the evidence for evolution. Are you aware of this happening with anyone? Why do you think this didn't happen to Todd?

4. What can the church do to better prepare its young people to maintain their faith and grow in Christ in a secular environment such as a public high school or university?

5. To what extent is your view of origins critical to your faith? If you could be convinced that your view of origins is wrong, how would that affect your faith?

CHAPTER 4

TOO GOOD TO BE TRUE

Darrel R. Falk

Though I am a bit older than Todd and grew up in Western Canada, in many ways, our childhoods were similar. I gave my heart to Jesus when I was four years old, after my sister caught me eating a peach I stole from a grocery store. One of my two earliest memories is tearfully kneeling beside a kitchen chair, telling Jesus I was sorry for having let him down by stealing a peach, asking him to forgive me, and inviting him to come into my heart. This was a serious conversion event, and I grew up loving my Christ-centered home, my church family, and especially my relationship with Jesus. Each night, my brother and I knelt by our beds in prayer, frequently falling asleep on our knees and needing to be placed in bed by our parents.

The idea of a God who cares intimately about me and the whole prospect of heaven were beautiful concepts to me. All in all, within my family and my church, my life was filled with joy, happiness, and love. There was a hymn in my old Nazarene church's hymnal with the phrase "safe and secure from all alarms," and that is an apt description of my childhood. I had a near perfect family life and church life.

And yet, I had my doubts. Outside of my church and family, I knew of hardly anyone who lived as serious Christians. If I had been born into a different family, I reasoned, I likely would not even believe in God, or at least not believe he is relevant in my life. If I had grown up in India, I would probably be Hindu. What were the odds that I could have been so fortunate as to have been born into the one correct religion when hardly anyone else in the world, apparently, was? These concerns were exacerbated by various experiences related to what seemed like conflicts between science and the Bible.

For example, as an eleven-year-old, I read the entire New Testament, and when I came to the book of Revelation and read that the angels would come from the "four corners of the earth," I knew that couldn't possibly be true because the earth is round. That really bothered me. The Bible, after all, is the Word of God. How could God, in his Word, get that detail wrong? Then in the seventh grade, I first encountered the theory of evolution in a social studies textbook. I saw the drawings of what prehumans were thought to look like and the time line that projected their gradual change toward humanness. The scientists were proposing something that didn't fit with what God's Word said about human origins, and they were doing so with fossils found on earth. These scientists were really intelligent. Could they all be wrong and the Bible right? I made it through this time partly by not allowing myself to dwell on these doubts and partly by exercising faith that answers to my questions would be forthcoming. At the end of seventh grade, I attended a summer camp and developed a close friendship with a couple of sixth graders. "Seventh grade social studies is really tough on your Christian faith," I told them. "You'll be doing very well if you make it through this next year with your faith intact." But I did make it, and my dedication to Christ remained strong, even though I yearned to be sure that God was real—I longed for some assurance. Early one summer morning, I lay in bed as the doubts welled up. I prayerfully asked God to show me he was real by wiggling the leaves on the cherry tree outside the window of my bedroom. They didn't wiggle. And once more I had to suppress doubts about whether there really is a God who "walks with me and talks with me," like the gospel song says so movingly. If that is true and not merely my imagination, surely he would be able to wiggle the cherry tree leaves to reassure me. But he didn't. So while my struggle produced its share of agony, I still strongly chose to believe in God and desired to live for him. I would come to understand it better by and by. With my inquisitive, analytical mind, it wasn't easy, though, and I couldn't ignore ideas that didn't ring true. I desperately wanted to know that God is real and was frustrated that the only way out of my dilemma was not to think about it.

No one in my family or church community knew about my struggle. I kept it secret throughout my late childhood and teenage years, partly because I was sure that no one would be able to say anything reassuring I didn't already know. But also, unfortunately, I was concerned that various individuals would think less of me and my Christian walk if they knew that there were times when I was secretly calling out to God, asking him to show me in some tangible way that he is real and not a figment of my imagination.

Unlike Todd, I was never really a science nerd in the sense of being fascinated with science. There were kids in my school who knew a lot about astronomy, electronics, or chemistry, but I wasn't one of them. Although I was not athletic either, I loved sports. I spent hours analyzing the statistics of the players in my baseball card collection, and my dream was to make my junior high school basketball team so that I could become a basketball star someday. My closest friend wanted to become a pro golfer, and his plan was to travel around the country preaching at revival meetings when he wasn't playing golf. Our heroes were Christian athletes, and we dreamed about being like them. As I got a little farther along in school, I knew I loved analytical disciplines, and thought maybe I would be an accountant or an engineer. I also liked the physical science courses I took, but stayed as far away from biology as I could, in no small part because that's where evolution reigned and I hated those faith-destroying doubts.

When it came time to go to college, I definitely wanted to go to a Christian college. I thought that it would strengthen my faith and bring me into a community that would facilitate the transition into adulthood as a Christian and not a skeptic. At the time, there were no Christian liberal arts colleges in Canada, and the cost of attending a Christian college in the United States was just too much for my parents to afford. I enrolled at Canadian Nazarene College, a Bible school that allowed for some of my credits to transfer. My plan was to attend there for a year, and while I hoped to be able to transfer to a Christian college in the States, I pretty much knew that I'd never be able to afford it. The best part about that plan, though, is that it was at Canadian Nazarene that I met my wife, Joyce. Of course, it also strengthened my knowledge and appreciation of the Bible.

Despite my desire to transfer to a Christian college,

I ended up going to a secular university near Vancouver. When I transferred from the Bible college to the university, I thought I might become a doctor, which led me to take a biology course, despite my concerns about evolution. As it turned out, the timing couldn't have been better. Up until then, biology was more descriptive than analytical, so from my perspective, it was just a requirement for becoming a doctor. But the field of biology was undergoing a tremendous change, becoming very analytical. The genetic code had just been discovered, and this discovery presented opportunities to use the analytical portion of my mind that in the past had been used largely for matters like baseball statistics and sorting through doubts about the Bible. The way that code worked to build organisms absolutely fascinated me. I yearned to know more, and the best way to do that was to take more biology courses and to change my career goal from being a physician to being a scientist.

During this time, my faith remained strong. I had recently gotten married to Joyce, and the year of Bible college as well as teaching some Sunday school kept me strong spiritually. The processes of life I was observing as a science student were so intricate and so beautiful that even if they were created through evolution (and I came to be quite certain they were), the process had to be God's and under God's control. Much to my surprise, going into biology strengthened and enriched my faith; I was now much better prepared to understand that the apparent conflicts between Scripture and science were likely caused by our interpretive limitations. I just knew that there had to be a God to create something so marvelous.

However, it was in the later stages of my graduate education at the University of Alberta that things changed. We were in a wonderful church and well supported by Christian friends, but I got caught up in the excitement of being part of an academic community and especially of the success I was experiencing as a young geneticist. The big question in genetics at that time was how in the world the information in genes gets transposed from double-stranded DNA molecules in a fertilized egg to the making of a complete adult organism with all of its intricately interacting parts. I loved doing the experiments that enabled me to advance knowledge in my own little sphere, learning small things about this broader question that no one else had ever known before. I was good at it, and it captivated me. We were just beginning to get exciting glimpses into possible tools that were needed to answer key parts of this great mystery of the ages: How does life unfold? The study of genetics with the goal of being a successful geneticist became the most important thing to me.

At the same time, I was abandoning some of the things I was taught growing up that had been important to me.

Earlier I had felt that there were good reasons not to go to movies; they were not conducive to a life of holiness, a life centered in the pursuit of God. I felt it was best not to be distracted by an industry geared toward a whole different set of values. I also had believed, given what I had seen of its abuse, that there was good reason to refrain from drinking alcohol. But in my new environment, no one thought that way, and eventually, right or wrong, neither did I. I was also quite pleased with my academic community, none of whom, as far as I could tell, were Christians. In my five years of graduate work and three years of postdoctoral fellowships, I never met any other biologist whom I knew to be a Christian. Late in my grad school years and early in my postdoc time, I became more and more irregular in Bible study and prayer, and finally I gave up that aspect of my life altogether. The Christian life, I felt, is grounded in Jesus' teaching about love, so why not just be a kind person? For that, it didn't matter anymore whether God exists, and given that I didn't know any fellow biologists who were committed to his existence as an explanation for life, I largely let the matter slide.

It was halfway through my first postdoctoral fellowship when I began to have second thoughts about my rejection of faith. By this time we had started our family and had two young daughters. I began thinking, almost in a panic, "I've thrown away all that was important to me—all the purpose and meaning that I once had. All for this academic life I'm living. I have two little girls now. Is this what I want for my family?" I also began questioning my career as a geneticist. "What if I fail? What if it doesn't turn out the way I hope it will? Where will I turn?" I realized I had left something really rich and I had better be sure I was replacing it with something better, and I concluded that I wasn't.

From my Bible training, I knew about the apostle Paul and his interactions with the Greeks at the Areopagus who were spending all of their time discussing the latest ideas but, at the end of the day, were left only with the possibility of an unknown god. I had been paying homage to the gods of humanism and secular advancement but was left feeling empty. If I passed that emptiness to my little girls rather than what I had known when I was a child, life for them would likely also lack meaning. Still filled with my doubts about faith, I did something which set the course of the rest of my life. I knelt down by my bed and told God that I wasn't sure he existed but that I wanted him to come back into my life. I told him that I would like to live as though he was real and then reassess things later. Thankfully, God was patient and gracious with me despite my reluctance to fully embrace him. I read great books by deeply engaging Christian thinkers, and I found that people much smarter than me had found

Christ's existence, the resurrection, and the life of faith highly persuasive. I walked and talked with God daily and loved the meaning with which my life was once more infused. Initially, I still wasn't sure he existed, but after two years of living in his presence by faith—and having so many profound experiences of that presence—he became real to me. Of this I was now certain.

However, I was a biologist now, and I had no doubt about the evolutionary process being the mechanism that God used to fulfill his creation command. Right or wrong, even though I enjoyed a close relationship with God, I felt there was no place for me in evangelical churches. Such churches, it seemed to me, had grown increasingly uncomfortable with the mainstream scientific account of creation. I recall a particular visit to the beach one Sunday afternoon when I saw a bus with the name of a Nazarene church on it. It appeared as if the youth group had been taken to the beach after church for a picnic. As I watched from a distance, I felt so sad that I would never be able to take my daughters to a church like that, where they learned Bible stories and sang choruses about Jesus and his love for them. Instead, we attended a quite liberal church while we were in California, a church that had no problem with my views on evolution but was unable to provide for me and my family what I had experienced as a child. I longed for a church where God's personal involvement in our lives was celebrated. I honestly believed that I would never be able to experience that again, and it broke my heart.

After completing my postdoctoral work, I joined the faculty of Syracuse University, and my hunger to be part of a dynamic church grew, along with the conviction that it would never happen. We were thousands of miles from friends and family, with no church which could enable us to experience what we wanted: an emphasis on a personal relationship with Christ without making us feel like second-class citizens because we accepted mainstream science. We tried a few churches, but none seemed to be a good fit, and after fourteen months in Syracuse, I had pretty much decided to give up on church, a decision that deeply troubled me because I knew the potential ramifications for my family.

I decided to give it one more try with a church on the far side of town. My wife and I had sat on a hill above the church one Sunday morning about six months earlier to watch the people as they left, wondering whether, despite its conservative nature, we might find a home there regardless of my being a scientist. But we concluded that it wouldn't work. Months later, and having given up on all other options, we decided to give it one last try before giving up on church altogether. Our plan was for me to go alone and not fill out any cards or make any kind of commitment, because we knew we probably wouldn't fit in.

So I went, and after the service I couldn't wait to get home to share what I had experienced. This was the church we were looking for and didn't think existed in Syracuse. It emphasized a personal relationship with Christ, and I sensed that no one would care that I was a scientist at the university and believed in evolution. They just loved us. Before long we joined the church, and I was teaching a Sunday school class of young adults. And our four- and six-year-old girls loved their Sunday school class and new friends. Discovering that church and the life in Christ we experienced there was so fulfilling that after seven years there, I felt called by God to leave Syracuse University and devote the rest of my life to the biology education of college students in an environment focused on Christian growth and nurture. Probably this was the greatest surprise of my life, and it led to fulfillment beyond anything I could have imagined.

I love science because I believe it points to a creator. A creator who loves us so much that he emptied himself of the royalty that he deserves in order to suffer an abandoned and unimaginably terrible death so that we might be brought near—into his outstretched arms. This love is the bond that holds Todd and me together despite our rigorous differences as scientists, differences that pale when we are both enfolded within those outstretched arms.

For Study and Reflection

1. Both Todd and Darrel grew up in small, conservative churches and in loving Christian families. Why do you think they have such different stories of continuing their higher education?

2. Darrel's strong childhood faith occasionally confronted doubts that he was afraid to share with his parents or other Christian adults. How could the church become a place where young people feel comfortable sharing their doubts, and how should older, mature Christians respond to young people who raise questions about the faith?

3. Many Christian young people who attend a secular university move away from the faith. Is this inevitable? Are there things the church could do to support these young people?

4. Would you encourage a young person to enter a science career where the vast majority of his or her colleagues would not be Christians and would see no reason to believe in God? Why or why not?

5. What was it that kept Darrel away from church in his adult life, and what was it that drew him back? What lessons can we learn from his experience?

ALL THINGS HOLD TOGETHER

Rob Barrett, The Colossian Forum

The Colossian Forum brought Todd and Darrel together because we believe Christians ought to be able to disagree over really serious issues yet still remain in the bonds of Christian love and fellowship. To put it another way, conflict offers Christians an opportunity to grow their love for God and for each other. We believe this because we believe the Bible when it teaches that in Christ "all things hold together" (Col. 1:17).

What does that really mean? That eventually either Darrel or Todd will win but they'll still be friends? Maybe, but we don't think that's what Scripture promises. And we really don't see either Todd or Darrel waving the white flag and saying, "You're right." Both believe deeply that they are contending for the truth, which is often what drives people to become passionate in their disagreements. The topic of origins has divided families, so we should not be surprised that Christians have a difficult time discussing it with each other. But remember those reassuring words of Paul: "all things hold together." If that's true, why do we have such a hard time with conflict?

At the risk of stating the obvious, we struggle with conflict because, well, it's hard. Messy. Uncomfortable. If I tell the truth, it might hurt someone's feelings. If I disagree with you, it might make you angry or defensive. Which is why too often we get to one of those heated, divisive moments and essentially bypass it with a group hug and a false hope that the conflict will somehow be miraculously resolved. That's not what the apostle had in mind when he instructed us that "all things hold together." He was simply reminding us that, as Christians, we have been given everything we need to live together as members of God's family regardless of the things that might otherwise drive us apart. We may even need our conflicts to drive us beyond ourselves to a place where we can be formed by Christlike virtues. Being "in Christ" means practicing those virtues of compassion, kindness, humility, gentleness, patience, and love (Col. 3:12–14). The issues that divide us might never be resolved this side of heaven, but we will still be able to experience true Christian unity right here and right now.

That sounds good on paper, but does it work?

CHAPTER 5

THIS WILL NEVER WORK

Todd Charles Wood

I did not want to meet with Darrel.

I was told that we would be provided a comfortable, nonthreatening environment where we would have an honest discussion about our opposing views of how the earth came into existence. We were also told that we would have to get into the really difficult issues that often create a lot of tension. That seemed a little redundant. I mean, how can you *not* get into the really difficult issues if the topic is evolution? I thought, "This will never work. There's just no way anything good will come out of this, so why bother?" That was quickly followed by fear. After all, I'd seen and heard about meetings like this. People were either superficially civil while stabbing each other in the back, or they just opened the floodgates of pent-up rage. I knew that no matter how much everyone tried to be nice to each other, this experiment would probably self-destruct. I didn't really want to be a part of that. If it didn't self-destruct, then it would be superficial and accomplish nothing. I didn't really want to waste my time on that either.

I began my professional career in 1994, right about the time the internet was becoming a household feature, and this newfangled "electronic mail" promised to revolutionize communication. The internet was a great way for creationists to network and exchange ideas with each other, but it also brought out the worst in people, especially anyone who disagreed with you. And critics of people like me were not shy about voicing their disdain and disgust for my creationist views. It wasn't difficult to shake off the barbs from scientists and others who professed no religious faith at all. Their attacks were predictable. What really disheartened me were the nasty comments from people who claimed to be Christians and taught at Christian colleges and universities.

At the same time, I understood why Christian evolutionists were so opposed to anyone who held a creationist point of view. A lot of what creationists have done to support their views is just bad science or not science at all. Because I am a creationist, I get painted with the same big ugly brush: if I believe the earth was created by God in six days a few thousand years ago, I couldn't possibly be a real scientist. After a while, you get tired of being treated like a fool, and I decided to just live and let live. The evolutionists could do their thing. I would do mine.

Then a few years ago, I was asked to attend a conference at a Christian college where one of their professors—an evolutionist—and I would explain why we believed what we did. For some reason, I ignored my usual reluctance to walk into the lions' den of ridicule I knew I would face and accepted the invitation. Unusually, the conference was organized and paid for by a guy who worked in the facilities department at the college. Not exactly a janitor but not the chairman of the science department either. He had observed the college embrace teaching evolution and felt led to at least give students some exposure to the young-age creationist point of view, a view that he held. As I understand it, the college wouldn't even let him hold the event on the campus but eventually decided to rent him their conference center, which was technically off campus. But he would have to pay for everything himself.

I arrived on campus trying my best to hide my nerves about the conference. I expected that the science faculty assumed that I was ignorant of evolution, like some kind of country bumpkin. I expected to be treated like the enemy. I met up with a professor from the college, who took me on a tour. He was very gracious and kind as he introduced me to his colleagues, and he seemed genuinely interested in me as a fellow believer. Spending some time to get to know him that afternoon helped me to be a little more at ease, even though I suspected we got along mostly by avoiding our differences.

The conference went fairly well. The professor made his presentation on evolution. I gave mine. I prattled on way too long because I really wanted to do a good job explaining my position. He asked some really good questions and seemed interested in my answers. He not only expressed interest in my research but also encouraged me to keep doing it. There were parts of the conference that weren't so fun, especially when another professor really epitomized the condescending arrogance I'd expected, but that was the exception. I have to admit that I kind of enjoyed it. I felt the audience actually took me seriously, even though by the end of the day they probably still thought I was nuts.

That conference really validated something I had thought for a long time: If people could see creationism done responsibly and well, then maybe they wouldn't react with scorn and mockery, like the internet trolls. They might even see that creationism isn't just based on a story in an ancient religious text but that there's science behind it. On the other hand, I wasn't at all convinced that the cordial response I received at that conference would be common. I am a young-age creationist, after all.

Which brings me back to Darrel. Despite that positive experience, I was still cautious, and I didn't want to meet with Darrel. I knew our hosts were going to force us to talk about the hard issues. There would be no chance to walk away. I couldn't just stop talking. We would have to spend an entire weekend together at a large bed-and-breakfast. I couldn't deflect the conversation with chitchat. I would have to sit and listen to whatever litany of complaints he had against me, and then I would have to state my own complaints.

Let's face it. Darrel isn't just a typical Christian evolutionist. He helped start BioLogos, an organization devoted to promoting the theory of evolution to as many Christians as possible. (They probably wouldn't describe their mission that way, but that's essentially what they do.) Some of the people involved in the formation of BioLogos had written scathing articles about creationists that only supported the stereotype of creationist stupidity. Darrel is basically the archenemy of young-age creationists! Why would I agree to enter enemy territory so that its commander in chief could continue the assault?

Maybe the biggest reason I didn't want to begin a relationship with Darrel is because this is more than just an academic issue over which we disagree. It's personal.

It's my life. My career. I've invested the last twenty years in something that has cost me a lot. I love science and research, but very few universities will hire someone with my specialty who also believes in creationism. Young-age creationism means a lot to me. Why go out of my way to engage yet another evolutionist who ultimately wants to silence me and destroy the work that I've done? I'm on a quest to show how science makes sense of the true history of creation. Why would I want to waste time and effort on an endeavor that wasn't going to accomplish much and would just create more hard feelings? Why should I bother with Darrel?

I decided to go ahead with our meeting for two reasons. First, I felt that it really was an opportunity to continue what I had done at the previous conference. I had the chance once again to show the serious and scholarly side of creationism that is too often unseen. It was a chance to be a testimony for the truth of creation, and Christians are supposed to be people of truth.

Second, I felt I had no other option as a Christian. After all, I really believe the Bible is true, and not just when it tells us that God created the heavens and the earth. First Corinthians 13:2 teaches that without love, I am nothing. Jesus tells me to love not just my neighbor but my enemies as well. With Darrel, there's no way around that. If there's anyone in Christianity who's my archenemy, it would have to be Darrel. So I have to love him, and I felt I should at least meet this enemy I was supposed to love.

This loving-my-enemy thing is a big challenge, though. I do not like what Darrel is doing to promote a theory that I believe contradicts Scripture. This is not a minor spat where we can agree to disagree, hug each other, and move on. On this important topic of origins, we are mortal enemies, yet I'm supposed to love him. What does that even mean, and how do you do it? To be honest, it would be a lot easier for me to just ignore Darrel and go back to my research.

After I finally met Darrel, I discovered that he's actually a nice guy. He's a soft-spoken gentleman with an engaging, almost bashful smile—almost grandfatherly, which I mean as a compliment. And I learned that he *is* a proud grandfather, and a loving husband who enjoys traveling to far-off places with his wife (kind of like I do). My reservations were put at ease in that first meeting.

Temporarily.

To this day I have no idea why, but it wasn't long into our discussion that he suggested that I don't really know science. I won't go into the details, but I remember thinking, "Here we go again." This is what so many Christian evolutionists do. Instead of taking me seriously as a scientist and listening to what I have to say, they fall back on that old idea that I must be a fool for questioning evolution. He didn't insult me in so many words, but what I heard was, "Now there, Todd, you just don't understand the *real* science."

I admit that I took pleasure in setting him straight. I reminded him that I have a strong background in evolutionary science and that the doctoral and postdoctoral work I've done at highly regarded secular universities was focused on evolutionary biology. I reminded him that I had been a member of the Society for Molecular Biology and Evolution almost as long as I'd belonged to the Creation Research Society. I reminded him that I taught a regular course in evolutionary biology and that I attended regular conferences of evolutionary biologists. When I finished my little speech, I said, "How much more study of evolution do I have to do?"

Then Darrel apologized. Humbly and with emotion in front of the same group that had heard him be so casually dismissive, he admitted that he was wrong and that I really did know a lot about evolution. He even admitted that what he said about my science was dumb for him to say.

I am accustomed to people disagreeing with me. I'm fully aware that my views on origins fall way outside the boundaries of conventional science, and I can live with that. I'm not out to prove that the theory of evolution is wrong but to keep digging for evidence to help me better understand the history of God's creation as it is outlined in Genesis. I've even gotten used to being unfairly criticized, even ridiculed. What I'm not accustomed to is having an evolutionist apologize to me. Not just any evolutionist but one who is a highly respected leader in the Christian evolutionist movement.

I agreed to a second meeting with Darrel.

For Study and Reflection

1. Why is it that in a free society such as ours, people are fearful of saying what they really believe? Can you think of examples of this?
2. At what point is it a waste of time to engage in a debate or discussion with someone you know disagrees with you? Explain.
3. A childhood saying goes, "Sticks and stones may break my bones, but words will never hurt me." Yet Todd was hurt by Darrel's words. Describe a situation where you either have hurt someone with your words or have been hurt by another's words. How was this situation resolved?
4. Think back on the last argument you had with someone close to you—spouse, son or daughter, close friend. What caused it to escalate? What eased the tension and made it more civil? How do you rate yourself in the way you disagree with those close to you?

5. Todd was surprised that Darrel apologized to him. Why do you think an apology from a fellow Christian was so surprising to him? Do you ever find it difficult to say, "I'm sorry"?

CHAPTER 6

RESCUED BY BROKENNESS

Darrel R. Falk

I really hadn't planned on meeting Todd or engaging in a face-to-face dialogue with him over a period of several years. Initially we were going to review a book together, he from his perspective as a young-earth creationist and I as an evolutionist. I had asked The Colossian Forum, a group that I knew was interested in bringing together Christians who have serious disagreements with each other, if they might host a dialogue in which Todd and I could use the book as a way to interact on the topic of origins, but as it turned out, Todd didn't feel comfortable meeting with me. Or at least interacting over the book I had suggested. I still feel bad about that because I'm sure some of his reluctance was based on the way many of us in the evolutionary creationist movement initially characterized those who believe in a literalistic interpretation of Genesis 1. Just as some unkind criticism has been aimed at evolutionary creationists from the young-earth creationist movement, I'm afraid that some Christians who believe in evolution have belittled the intellect of young-earth creationists. My thought at the time was that Todd did not want to subject himself to criticism that was either unfair or harsh.

Eventually, however, Todd, though still reluctant or maybe even a little suspicious, had a change of heart, so in July of 2013, we met for the first time along with several others—science skeptics like Todd and mainstream science supporters like me. The plan was to meet in the evening for dinner at a nice restaurant so that we could get to know each other before discussing our views of origins. We began our time around the dinner table sharing our testimonies. For the next two and a half hours, we each recounted our journeys with the Lord and how our respective views of origins grew out of our love for God. It really was a wonderful experience, and I think we were able to see each other first as Christ-followers with a great deal in common rather than as advocates of opposing viewpoints. It reminded me of Jesus' words in Matthew: "For where two or three gather in my name, there am I with them" (18:20). I think we all sensed the Lord's presence around the table in that restaurant, and I went back to my room encouraged and eager to engage with these fellow Christians the next day on a topic that has been so divisive for the church.

We gathered the next morning, and the format allowed for Todd and me to explain our views of origins, followed by the opportunity to critique each other. Our dialogue was fairly direct, yet respectful. However, at one point I said that Todd did not adequately understand evolutionary theory. In front of our small group, I told him that I thought his views were shaped by his having attended the fundamentalist Liberty University and said something to the effect that if he had gone to a mainstream university, he might look at evolution differently. I said that Todd did not have a thorough understanding of evolutionary theory and that his position had not been carefully and studiously developed. I really believed this to be true and felt that it was important to get my thoughts out in the open. I wasn't trying to put him down; I just thought that we needed to be honest with one another. Still, my comments put a damper on the whole conversation, and I came to realize not only that I had been too frank for this stage of our time together but also that I was just plain wrong. Todd regularly attended the annual meeting of the society of evolutionary biologists. Not only did he understand evolutionary theory quite well, he likely knew it better than me. He just thought it was wrong.

To his credit, Todd listened politely, and although I could see that he thought I was wrong, I knew that my blunt evaluation had hurt him. I left the session with a heaviness of heart that troubled me, especially since the more I thought about it, the more I knew I was wrong. As I was making my statement, I had forgotten that Todd had earlier told us about his attendance at the evolution society meetings. The more I reflected, the more I remembered the high scientific quality of some of Todd's work that I had read about. I knew I had to apologize and that I needed to do it just as I had spoken so carelessly about him: in front of our group. When we gathered for our next session, I asked for a few moments to speak before we began with our agenda and used that time to try to undo the damage I knew I had done to our relationship. I confessed my error of mischaracterizing his background and apologized. I told him—and the others—that I admired his academic credentials as a scientist and never should have said what I had said. And I asked him to forgive me. It is a further tribute to Todd's integrity and graciousness that he accepted my apology and quickly forgave me.

In a way, it was probably a good thing that this unfortunate incident happened the way it did. So many times in our church circles we are afraid to admit we're wrong, digging in our heels and further dividing the body of Christ. Or when we feel we've been treated unfairly, we retreat into resentment or retribution, which Todd easily could have done. But if we follow the Spirit's leading in those moments of failure, we can experience the healing that he desires for us.

Our first meeting could have ended our relationship, but instead it set the stage for our second meeting, which was held on the campus where I taught, Point Loma Nazarene University. From the very beginning, I sensed some tension in the air. I also knew that Todd was going through a difficult time because it looked like his position where he taught was going to be eliminated. By this time, I had grown to really care for Todd, so knowing what he was going through drew me even closer to him.

But the tension I sensed wasn't necessarily about him but about another young-earth creationist in attendance, a friend of mine with whom I'd had lunch on several occasions. I loved this guy, but he was different from Todd in one respect. He didn't have a biology background at all, but because of some books that he'd read, he probably felt a little too confident about his knowledge of evolutionary science. When his turn to talk came, his high level of confidence resulted in his saying some things that were as naively wrong as I had been in my comments about Todd. One of my colleagues, who also held the same position on origins that I did, was deeply offended by his statements and decided to confront him pretty directly. "You have just insulted me," she said. "You just told me that everything I do and think is wrong, and you've implied that I am a naive and very poor thinker." He apologized profusely, and despite his naivete about science and the mistake he had made in putting down others who think differently, the Spirit of Christ brought wonderful healing to the situation. Still, both Todd and I knew how wrong he had been about some of his scientific statements, and it brought the two of us closer together. In a sense, we felt we were on the same side, but the conversation had become so infused with the Holy Spirit's presence that it was almost as though there weren't two sides. We were all, in a meaningful way, enjoying exploring our differences together.

The next morning, we met at a little restaurant for breakfast, and it was then that the Spirit of God worked in our hearts in a way that I think each of us considered to be miraculous. I can't remember whether it was my evolutionary creation colleague or my overly confident young-earth creation brother (he always called me brother—and meant it), but one of them suggested that we should go around the table and pray for each other. There were tears as we lifted each other up in prayer and experienced God's presence flowing in and through us. At one point, I was so overwhelmed by how much I cared about Todd, given some of the difficulties I knew he faced, that as I tried to express that to him and the others, I broke down and cried. Here we were, two people who vigorously disagreed with each other, yet because of God's Spirit we were able to address those disagreements not only with kindness and respect but with a tenderness that we rarely see among people who disagree with each other. I really wasn't expecting to care for Todd so much as a person. In those sacred moments of praying for each other, he was no longer someone with whom I disagreed but a real brother whom I loved.

This became the pattern for the remainder of our time together in that meeting. It wasn't just Todd and me, it was all eight or nine of us at that meeting. We would explore each other's positions, ask tough questions, reach a place where tension and unease settled in over us, and then God's Spirit would intervene. We would stop and pray for each other, read Scripture together, even sing together. It was through those practices that we were able to recognize again that the bonds of Christian love that connect us all are real and that we can trust them to be present even in the face of conflict.

By the end of that meeting, I felt that Todd and I had really developed a close and trusting relationship. We seemed to be on the same page in terms of continuing our discussion. I thought we both agreed that we'd get down to the scientific nitty-gritty of the difference between our two positions. It was at this time that a book was published by Graeme Finlay, a Christian geneticist in New Zealand. As I saw it, this book made rock solid the case that God created through the evolutionary process. I could not imagine any other explanation for the vast amount of data that he laid out. So, thinking that what Todd also wanted was a scientific discussion, I was anxious to see what he thought about it. It seemed to me to be a perfect way to advance our discussion. The goal of our meetings all along had been not to prove that either of us is right or wrong but to learn more about why we disagree, as well as to explore how even in conflict, Christ can be present. On this topic, it seemed to me that we couldn't really do that without addressing the science questions. Unfortunately, I must have misunderstood Todd. He wasn't interested in talking about this book at all, even though it was presenting data that was in our common area of expertise—genetics. This was very frustrating for me, but I now know that the reason he didn't want to talk about it is that although he knows the evidence is very strong, he believes that it is wrong and that we are too scientifically naive at this point to address the question of why—it just is. The Bible says so, he thinks, and that's his one and only authority. Todd is the first to acknowledge that there isn't enough scientific evidence yet to support young-earth creationism. There's some, he thinks, but he knows it is not nearly as much evidence as that for evolutionary creation.

The bigger issue for Todd, as I say, is the Bible. We both believe the Bible is authoritative and true. We just read the early chapters of Genesis differently.

─────── For Study and Reflection ───────

1. Can you think of examples either in your church experiences or in the culture at large of someone belittling those who look, think, or act differently from them or simply disagree with them? What do you think leads people to belittle others?
2. Darrel acknowledged that he misunderstood Todd, which led to his inaccurate and hurtful statement. To what extent are our differences compounded by our failure to understand others?
3. Think of someone you know who you feel is wrong about something. What specific steps could you take to better understand that person?
4. Which do you think is more difficult to do: ask for forgiveness or offer forgiveness? Explain.
5. What role can prayer play when individuals or parties find themselves in serious conflict?

SHAPED BY GOD'S LOVE

Rob Barrett, The Colossian Forum

Early on it became clear that something special was going on with Darrel and Todd. Trying to talk across a disagreement was nothing new, but these two scientists on opposite sides of a seemingly impenetrable wall somehow managed to persevere, even when things looked like they might fall apart. Undoubtedly, Darrel and Todd are Christians of unusual character. But good, Christian folk have tried this before and failed. One leader in the origins debate declined to join this project, and he shared his reasons with us. He had tried to connect with people on the other side, and it hadn't gone well. He wrote in a letter, "We always began each meeting with fellowship, biblical encouragement, and a time of prayer together. The atmosphere was always cordial and collegial. . . . I have given a serious effort to understand the positions, purposes, and passions of those who do not share [my] commitment [on origins]. I have cancelled any further participation in those meetings. I saw no progress and, indeed, a growing distance and hardening of personal angst that could not possibly produce anything positive."

In his experience, talking, praying, and trying to understand led only to increasing tensions. It was so bad that he concluded that meeting across the divide "could not possibly produce anything positive."

Why did it seem that Todd and Darrel were experiencing something positive? I had to conclude that God was doing something unusual. We couldn't orchestrate this ourselves. There was no technique or formula that could produce those precious moments of forgiveness after an offense.

Time and time again, these two bright scientists and devoted followers of Christ reached one of those places where you weren't sure how they would get through it. But they always did because the Holy Spirit seemed to bring them through. I know that sounds simplistic, but I believe it's God's nature to be with us in the midst of conflict. Once, toward the end of one of their meetings when they had really gotten into some difficult territory, Todd said, "I keep coming back because something's going on here, and I'm not real sure what it is and I don't know where it's going to take us, but it's exciting." What they experienced is the truth of the gospel right where they didn't expect to find it: right in the center of conflict.

Yet there was also something different about how we from The Colossian Forum, in concert with the scientists, were approaching these meetings. As we thought together about the conflict we were facing, we turned the problem upside down. We decided to focus first on loving God and loving each other, and only second on resolving the conflict. Or maybe it would be better to say that we were all determined to try to love God and each another at the very same time we stepped into the conflict. When questioned about the most important commandment, Jesus pointed to love of God and neighbor as the critical starting point. He went on to say, "All the Law and the Prophets hang on these two commandments" (Matt. 22:40). If everything hangs on these two things, maybe the battle over evolution does too. Maybe practicing the basics of Jesus' teaching provides a way through the mess. Christians of previous generations used to say, "God works in mysterious ways," yet they—and we—do not always trust those ways. Could asking for forgiveness when we've offended a brother be mysteriously linked to resolving the controversy over evolution? That just might be crazy enough to be exactly what the Holy Spirit would do.

If the church is going to adequately address divisive

issues, it will take more than clever insights into those issues. We need imaginations that have been calibrated to the shape of God's love. This happens not by chance but through practice. Praying together. Seeking the fruit of the Spirit even as we disagree. Reading God's Word together.

Ah—God's Word. Yet another challenge for Darrel and Todd. Both believe the Bible. Both believe the Bible is in harmony with their understanding of how God created. And both believe the other is wrong about the Bible, and among evangelical Christians, those are serious charges. Worth fighting over.

CHAPTER 7

GENESIS IS HISTORY

Todd Charles Wood

D arrel is right when he says that the big issue for me is the Bible, not science, but it goes much deeper than that. As a scientist, I think science is extremely important, but I don't think Christians ought to divorce their science from their faith, as if we could hold back something from the authority of Christ. That was the strategy of the Enlightenment and the Scientific Revolution. People thought it would be great to do science without consulting Scripture. Reason and evidence were supposed to be able to establish the Christian faith all by themselves. Today, we call it "methodological naturalism," this exclusion of God from science.

Think about what that means. I'm a Christian. I'm a slave to Christ. There's no part of my life that Jesus does not claim as his. My soul doesn't have a man cave where I can retreat and do what I want. I'm not a Christian on Sunday and a scientist on Monday. That's not how the Christian life works. For a little while, I might be able to do a thought experiment about what things might be like without my faith, but eventually that thought experiment has to come back under the sovereignty of my Savior.

So the idea of doing science as if God did not reveal himself in the Bible is incomprehensible to me. Even more, if you try it, you're going to go really wrong. Darrel looks at science today and sees such a powerful model of evolution that explains the history of life on this planet, and he does not see this as being incompatible with Christian theology. I look at modern science, and I see discord and confusion created by a process that never intended to consider God in the first place. Sounds crazy, but science needs to be redone. I don't doubt we'll keep a lot of science, and I wouldn't be surprised if we discover mistaken interpretations of Genesis along the way. But we can't make those decisions by doing science in isolation from Scripture or by interpreting Scripture in isolation from science. They have to go hand in hand. Jesus must be Lord of all.

How do we do this? It seems impossible to me. Science is such a massive thing in the modern world, and it overshadows everything we do. How can we twenty-first-century Christians separate the practice of science from the conclusions of four hundred years of research? Just as important as rethinking science is reexamining Scripture, and again, how can we do that with all of our scientific bias and baggage?

I believe we have reason to hope. First, we have Jesus' promise that the Holy Spirit will lead us into all truth. We really have to ponder that; we are not left to our own devices to figure out what is true. Second, I think we need to give up our egotistical notions that we already have all of the answers. Whether we're talking about science or the Bible, there are many unanswered questions. We've barely begun to chip away the thinnest surface of human ignorance. There will be some things we can feel certain about, but there will be many, many more that are blank slates. Third, with our faith intact and our egos in check, we can boldly approach the task before us, one piece at a time. Forget about scientific revolutions. This is going to take lots of little steps before that big breakthrough. This is going to take patience.

So what do we do with Genesis? Before I can answer that, it's important to think more carefully about what we do with the Bible in general. First and most important, as a Christian, I have to confess that the Bible is not merely a collection of ancient literature. The Bible is God-breathed, inerrant revelation from the Holy Spirit. We can talk about genres and authorial intent, and that can yield important insights. But at the end of that discussion, the Word of God is just that. God's authorship must be considered.

I've been rebuked for my view of the Bible by Darrel's colleagues. I've been told that my view makes the Scripture some kind of sacred, magical book removed from regular literary analysis. I respond, yes, that is exactly right. The Bible cannot be treated like any other form of literature because it *isn't* just any other form of literature. That doesn't make it untouchable. That doesn't mean we can't talk about literary form or genre or figures of speech or any of the other insights we can gain from literary analysis. It does mean that we can't treat texts in isolation, as if Genesis 1–11 could be excised from the rest of Scripture and treated like a separate unit. It also means that any imaginative reinterpretation of one passage that disrupts too many other passages must be treated with suspicion.

My second important consideration for understanding Scripture is the Protestant doctrine of perspicuity: when the Bible speaks clearly on a subject, it does so infallibly and with absolute authority. This is not some aberrant, modern doctrinal innovation. This has been standard Reformation teaching for five hundred years. On the other hand, we also must recognize the details of this doctrine. Traditionally, perspicuity means that the teachings *necessary for salvation* are clear, not that everything in the Bible is perfectly understandable. Some passages in the Bible are hard to understand. Nevertheless, a friend of mine who is an Old Testament scholar once told me that we ought to be as clear as the Bible is clear and as ambiguous as the Bible is ambiguous.

Unfortunately, a full treatment of my views on Genesis would require a book much longer than this one, so let's just skip to the conclusion: I read Genesis as largely describing history. Genesis describes real events that really happened in real time. That doesn't deny any of the rich, important theological truths communicated in Genesis. History and theology go hand in hand, as the apostle Paul explained when he described the history recorded in the Old Testament: "These things happened to them as examples and were written down as warnings for us" (1 Cor. 10:11). He makes it quite clear that the events are historical ("these things happened") and theological ("as examples and . . . warnings for us").

As I look at Genesis, it seems to have discrete units that present what appear to be historical narratives. Genesis 1 gives us the six days of creation. Genesis 2–4 gives us Adam and Eve and the fall, the first murder, and the spread of Cain's family. Genesis 5 is a single unit of genealogy stretching from Adam to Noah. Genesis 6–9 is the story of the flood; then chapter 10 provides us with the table of nations, where things are divided by clan and language. And then in Genesis 11 we rewind a bit and learn about Babel and where all those clans and languages came from.

If you read those chapters right now, you would see that the language is pretty straightforward. God created. God made. God rested. Adam did this. Noah did that. The text seems clear. But Darrel and his colleagues do not think this creation account happened the way it was recorded in the Bible. To them, it's a kind of allegory. God was speaking metaphorically here. They say that other parts of the Bible that look very similar to Genesis 1–11 are more historically and factually accurate, but here, for some reason, it's not.

Viewing those straightforward stories of Genesis as myth or allegory has a big ripple effect on the rest of Scripture. If Genesis 1–11 is not historical, why do we later read in the Ten Commandments that "in six days the Lord made the heavens and the earth"? If creation is ancient, why does the Bible read as if everything is very young? Why in the Gospel of Mark did Jesus say that marriage began "at the beginning of creation," which confirms that humans and all of creation started at the same time? It seems pretty clear to me that the Bible's message about creation is consistent throughout the text and records a historical account of what happened. Does it make sense from the perspective of modern science? Maybe not, or at least not yet. But the Bible contains a lot of things that don't necessarily add up, yet we still believe them.

Scientists like Darrel like to point to the weight of scientific evidence that the earth is old and life evolved, from which they conclude that we need to change the way we read the Bible. If the preponderance of evidence suggests that the earth has to be more than a few thousand years old, the biblical account must not be historically accurate. God must have been using metaphorical language or the genre of myth or allegory, because Genesis 1 just isn't scientifically accurate. So what are the rules? How do we know when to read the Bible as allegory and when to read it as history? Darrel clearly accepts as fact many other miracles in the Bible. Why not the miracle of a six-day creation or a global flood? What are the criteria for rejecting one miracle and accepting another? I've asked him, and I've never gotten a satisfactory answer other than he accepts the historicity of the Bible unless there's a "really good reason" to interpret the text some other way. What does that even mean? What's a really good reason?

I'm actually bothered more by *why* Christian evolutionists interpret Genesis the way they do than by the conclusions they eventually come to. Why is it that evangelical scholars are allowed and even encouraged to propose new interpretations of Genesis, but when my creationist colleagues and I propose new interpretations of science, we are shouted down? Why are the conclusions of modern science untouchable? Why invent increasingly improbable readings of Scripture? Shouldn't we be allowed to at least explore how well the evidence of creation might fit a traditional, historical reading of Genesis? If we really are scientists who trust the Bible, shouldn't we dig deeper into both the Scripture *and* the data? Shouldn't we approach the data of science with a bit more skepticism?

I should add that it makes me just as uncomfortable when Christians who hold to a creationist view ignore science. There are people who believe that nothing that comes from science will change the way they believe. Every single thing they learned in Sunday school must be defended. When I was growing up, the vapor canopy theory was popular, but that idea has been abandoned by most creation scientists I know. As it turns out, it wasn't worth defending. Here's where I agree with Darrel: when creationists ignore science or do not engage it seriously, it reinforces the view among secular scientists that Christianity has no place in science.

Whenever there appear to be conflicts between the Bible and science, Christians have an option that in my opinion is better than automatically changing our theology to accommodate science or ignoring science entirely, and that is to dig deeper into the science.

As for me, I am confident that Genesis 1–11 does give

a general account of the earliest events of the history of creation. If that's so, then certain scientific models (like evolution or the big bang theory) must be reinterpreted. We also need to recognize that evolutionists have come up with a lot of data that on the surface makes a strong case for their theory. Instead of dismissing it, we need to come up with a better explanation of the data. We need to ask honest questions and search hard for the answers. If we have not evolved from apes, why did God make us with such strong resemblance to apes? If Neanderthals are not our cousins, then what are they? If light from distant stars doesn't confirm that the universe is billions of years old, what *does* it tell us? These are legitimate questions that creation scientists should be asking. As a scientist who believes the Bible is true, I am not bothered by the evidence for evolution. Rather, it encourages me to try to understand what's really going on in God's creation, because I believe if we are faithful, God will always lead us to the truth.

Whatever the answers are to these complicated questions of science and Genesis, I always come back to my simple faith in God's Word. If I accept what Darrel is saying, then I have to admit that a very clear part of Scripture doesn't mean what it actually says. So how can I be certain that any of the rest of it means what it says? It's far easier for me to explore all the other ways of reading the data of science than to overturn a clear passage of Scripture.

—————— **For Study and Reflection** ——————

1. Todd tends to read the Bible—especially the early chapters of Genesis—as a newspaper or history book. How does this correspond to the way you read the Bible?

2. Todd thinks that people who read the early chapters of Genesis as allegory or myth do so because they want to make the Bible fit their view of science. Is this a fair criticism? Can you think of other ways that Christians may change their understanding of what the Bible teaches to make it fit contemporary culture?

3. Todd acknowledges much of the evidence for evolution but believes that if we continue to dig deeper into both Scripture and science, we will discover that the Genesis account is literally true. Why do you think we have not found that evidence yet?

4. What are the dangers of reading the Bible as Todd does—regarding it primarily as literal truth?

5. How can families who accept Genesis 1 as literal prepare their children to engage and respond to evolution?

CHAPTER 8

STORIES CAN BE TRUE

Darrel R. Falk

As we got to know each other better, I think Todd and I were somewhat surprised at how similarly we think about Scripture. What I mean by that is that we both affirm its truthfulness. Both of us are able to say that we believe the Bible; we believe that it is trustworthy and that through it God is speaking to us, instructing us, and guiding us into a right relationship with him. We both can affirm the truth of Genesis 1:1: "In the beginning God created the heavens and the earth."

But in practice, Todd and I approach Genesis 1–11 quite differently. Todd tends to read the Bible like most of us read the newspaper or a history book. To him, it is a collection of facts, an accurate and literal account of how God entered into a relationship with us, beginning with the creation and continuing to the resurrection and the eventual return of Christ to "judge the living and the dead" and to establish his kingdom, "which shall have no end." If I understand Todd correctly, he believes that even those things which seem impossible or improbable happened pretty much as described. So of course when he reads in Genesis that God created the earth in six days, he accepts that literally. And when he gets to the genealogies, he does the math and concludes that the earth is quite young. Therefore, he cannot accept the theory of evolution because the Bible describes the origin of the earth and everything in it differently.

This, perhaps, is the fundamental difference between Todd and me. I don't read Genesis 1–11 in the same way I read a newspaper. Instead, I read it as a story, a narrative given to us in a way that we can understand what God is doing in the world and in us. Sometimes, the Bible is a historical report of actual events that happened in biblical times. But I think sometimes, such as in Genesis 1, the Bible employs metaphorical language to reveal its truth. So when I read it, I'm not so much concerned whether, for example, there was a real garden of Eden and a serpent and a forbidden fruit. There may have been, but it would not upset me if sometime in eternity I discover that what we know as "the fall of man" did not occur precisely as described in Genesis 3. Instead, as I read the Bible, I'm always asking myself, "What is God trying to say to us in this passage?" Whether or not there was a serpent and an apple, the account of the fall teaches me the important truth about my sinful nature and vulnerability to temptation. I am very comfortable with the existence of two specific archetypal individuals, Adam and Eve, singled out from among others present to enter into relationship with God in the way that N. T. Wright, John Walton, and Scot McKnight describe. Given that Paul, and Jesus himself, reference Adam and Eve as historical individuals, this seems to make sense, and there is no scientific data that is inconsistent with the view put forward by these writers. We do know from genetics that there was never a time when just two members of our species were present on earth. But even Scripture hints at that. (For example, did Cain marry his sister, and if so, why doesn't the narrative mention that?)

The factual accuracy of Genesis 1–11 isn't as important to me as God's message. What's most important to me is what God is revealing to us in the story of Adam and Eve in the garden of Eden: he lovingly created us to be in relationship with each other and in relationship with him. However, out of love, God also created us with freedom to choose. Adam and Eve yielded to the temptation to be "like God," to be the masters of their own destinies, rather than following on the pathway set out for them by God. As a result, instead of living "naked and unashamed" before God, they felt the need to cover up, to hide from God, and thereby entered into a life of shame and guilt before God. The story of Adam and Eve is more than the story of the first couple who lived in relationship with God; it is our story too. We have the freedom to choose to be "like God," making our own decisions about what we want to do, rather than living out of our covenant with our Creator. The Tree of Life, as Dietrich Bonhoeffer states so beautifully in *Creation and Fall*, reappears again in the Gospels, and on that tree, to which we once again can have access, is the Christ who dies so that humankind can have life and "have it more abundantly." Much more can be said and indeed has been said in some of my favorite books, but the point is that the story of Adam and Eve is so much more than a history lesson. I think Todd and I largely agree even here, but I am not concerned about whether there really was a talking snake, whether Eve literally was created out of Adam's side, or even whether there was a single real tree that tested their obedience. I am more interested in the everlasting truths of the story.

The same is true for Genesis 1. This is a story so true that it needs to be expressed through imagery, not as a scientifically testable eyewitness account.

Even though I do not read Genesis 1–11 the same way I would read the newspaper or a textbook, I believe that Todd and I both look at its message in a similar way. He just thinks that the entire account is meant to convey real history as well, and I don't. I think we both agree that Genesis 1 teaches us that God is the Creator of the universe and created all that exists. It paints this big, beautiful picture of the God of the cosmos and the majesty of the created universe. It counters the view of other cultures that there are other gods, even that the sun and the moon are gods. Genesis 1 says, "No, there is but one God, the God of Israel, and he created everything else, including the sun and the moon." It creates this sense of awe as to who God is.

Then we come to Genesis 2 and 3, and we see a different picture of God. Where in the previous chapter he was this all-powerful and mighty Creator of the universe, we now see him bending down and picking up a handful of dirt to form man. I see this as a beautiful image that reveals a God who loves and cares for individuals. A personal God. The God of the universe also loves and cares for each of us personally. There's something deeply moving about placing those two views of God side by side. The picture of the Creator who loved into existence two people, talking to them, creating a beautiful garden for them, giving them a perfect world with everything they needed to be happy, not only suggests a kind and loving God but gives us a peek at what we can look forward to, which we see in the book of Revelation: a return to the perfect world God desires for us, but which we can begin to enter through Christ and the power of his resurrection.

My concern is that when many people read the Bible as they would read a newspaper or textbook, it seems to me they can get so caught up in the details of its factual accuracy that they miss God's message. I'm not suggesting that Todd does this, but I see a tendency to put more emphasis on trying to convince people that, for example, a serpent actually talked than on understanding and appreciating what God is telling us. I do not have to believe every detail of what happened in the garden to accept and apply the message that comes from that passage of the Bible. As I explained in my book, *Coming to Peace with Science*, the apostle Paul teaches that great truths about God often come from revelation rather than human wisdom. Or as Paul puts it, we understand what God has given us "in words taught by the Spirit, expressing spiritual realities with Spirit-taught words" (1 Cor. 2:11–13).

Why is this way of reading Genesis 1–11 so important to me? As I described earlier, even as a youngster I had difficulty reconciling what I pretty much knew to be true with some of what I read in the Bible that didn't seem to be accurate. In Isaiah and again in Revelation, the Bible mentions "the four corners of the earth." I knew this couldn't be true, and it was the cause of some innocent childhood doubt. I need to be clear and admit that my later wandering from the faith was not entirely caused by such doubts. At that point, I didn't really care about the Bible all that much but had put my career ahead of everything, including God. However, many in the scientific community and the culture at large reject our faith when they are led to believe they must accept the Genesis account of creation as being literally true. They simply are unable to ignore or dismiss the volumes of evidence that counter the "facts" of young-earth creationism.

They don't have to. They can read these passages in Genesis as I do, as a beautiful and engaging narrative of how a Creator God who gives life to everything loves us and longs to have a relationship with us. It is a story that begins in a garden and ends in a garden-city where we can live with him forever. It is the story of the human condition, of how we choose to be our own gods but can be grace-fully rescued from that condition by the sacrifice of the Son, who "emptied himself, taking the form of a slave . . . humbled himself and became obedient to the point of death—even death on a cross" (Phil. 2:7–8 NRSV). That's the theme of the creation story in its completeness, which is why I can say that even though Todd and I read this portion of the Bible differently, we agree on its message and that the world desperately needs to hear that message. I love God's Word and trust it completely.

And I want others to see that they can trust it too. Helping them focus on the message rather than the scientific accuracy of the text will help them do that.

I realize that what I have just written may be disturbing to some—that the way I read these passages is no different from, and may be influenced by, liberal scholars who do not consider the Bible to be the uniquely revealed Word of God. If I read Genesis as a metaphor for the way God created the universe, what prevents me from eventually deciding that the resurrection is similarly a story that never really happened?

Fair concerns. Theological liberalism tends to have a somewhat low view of Scripture—seen as merely the account of one nation, Israel, and its interactions with God. Theological liberalism also downplays and, in some cases, denies the notion of God reaching down to save humankind, replacing that beautiful story of redemption and grace with the responsibility of humans to change society through their own efforts.

As an evangelical Christian, I fully accept the Bible as God's inspired account of how he interacts with us. Its message offers instruction and guidance for the way God wants us to live, which is in a personal relationship with him. I still have a responsibility to influence society and make it better, but I know that this can happen only through the power of the Holy Spirit working in and through me. With the exception of the early chapters in Genesis, science cannot prove or disprove singular events such as God inscribing the Ten Commandments on a stone tablet, Jesus turning water into wine, or the resurrection, and that is where faith comes in. I believe the Bible is true. I believe we can trust its message, its teaching about how to live and how to treat others.

The Bible is so much more than a newspaper or a textbook. It is far richer and deeper than a collection of scientific facts about the age of the earth. When I listen for the message that God is trying to tell me on each page of the Bible, I hear a unique and beautiful story that leads me always to God and invites me to participate in his plan of salvation for sinful humankind.

I have learned that Todd reads Scripture the same way. Our primary difference is how literally we take those early chapters of Genesis. Both of us arrive at the same place when it comes to the message of love and redemption that God has for all humankind.

For Study and Reflection

1. Darrel reads the Bible more as a collection of stories, some factual, some allegorical. How do you read the Bible? What concerns do you have with those who read it differently than you do?

2. In what ways are Todd and Darrel in agreement over the Bible?

3. Do you agree with Darrel that the most important aspect of reading the Bible is to hear and respond to its message, not to get caught up in the details? Why or why not?

4. What are the dangers in reading the Bible as Darrel does—seeing some things as allegory rather than historical fact?

5. For Christian families who want to be faithful to the Bible and who read it as Darrel does, how should children be taught about Genesis? At what age should they be taught that God didn't create the world exactly as described in Genesis 1?

THE SCIENCE BEHIND THE THEOLOGY

Rob Barrett, The Colossian Forum

When it comes to the science of origins, Darrel appears to hold all of the cards. Legions of scientists have been working diligently for more than a century to refine our understanding of evolution. Mountains of evidence support the theory of evolution, so much that no single scientific specialist can appreciate it all. Even Todd would agree with that.

But one thing about scientific study is that there are always some observations that don't fit the current theory so well. Sometimes these inconsistencies are just mistakes or misunderstandings. But it's not at all uncommon for the prevailing scientific theory to need adjusting here or there. Many scientists ignore the occasional unusual result, while others grasp hold of them as the leading edge of something important. In the early 1900s there were some niggling experimental results that didn't fit the theories of physics at the time. Some creative and persistent scientists worked hard on those problems and, lo and behold, the new physics of relativity and quantum mechanics was born.

Todd is the kind of scientist who focuses on the little discrepancies. He's one of a very small handful of young-earth creationists who accept much of the evidence for evolution, and he doesn't spend much time trying to refute it. Instead, he's using his skills and knowledge as a scientist to press hard on the exceptions that he believes provide a starting point for building a case for a young earth created in six days. He would be the first to admit that so far, he has not made significant progress, but Todd believes that convincing evidence for a young earth will inevitably surface. His understanding of the Bible demands it and he wants to be part of finding it. Darrel believes that any remaining difficulties with evolutionary theory will be explained through the normal scientific process. He thinks it's incredibly unlikely that science will come to see the theory of evolution as a giant mistake.

As Christians and as scientists, both Todd and Darrel are committed to speaking honestly about what they know and what they don't. That's not always easy to do. They each have reconciled their faith with their science, but in different ways. Darrel accepts the evidence for evolution and sees it as completely compatible with his faith. Todd accepts the historical accuracy of Genesis and does not see that at odds with science.

If we're going to get to know these two men and their conflict, we have to wade into their scientific expertise. I know the language and concepts of science can be intimidatingly unfamiliar and complex for the average layperson. No matter how exciting Darrel and Todd find these matters, for some the details can seem mind-numbingly dull. So I asked our scientists to unpack their scientific explanations of origins in as simple a manner as possible without being simplistic. For those who would appreciate a more complete treatment of the science behind their views, I refer you to Darrel's book, *Coming to Peace with Science* (IVP Academic), as well as his YouTube channel— *Coming to Peace with Science with Darrel Falk*, and to the website *www.humangenesis.org*, which Todd edits.

CHAPTER 9

OVERWHELMING EVIDENCE

Darrel R. Falk

Although the work of scientists can seem complex and confusing to some, it is really pretty simple. We basically observe things and try to explain what we see. Based upon what we see, we develop a hypothesis to explain our observations. This hypothesis leads to certain predictions—"if so and so is correct, we would expect such and such." We then develop tests to see whether the predictions hold up. If they don't, our hypothesis is wrong. If they do, it may be right. Eventually, when lots of predictions have been tested, and none have been shown to be wrong, scientists reach the conclusion that the hypothesis is likely correct.

Darwin's theory of evolution through the process of natural selection is broader than one hypothesis. It is an all-encompassing attempt to explain the origin of life's diversity. Over the past 150 years, it has led to many hypotheses. Here is one example. If evolution is true, there would be a time when there would have been a lineage from fish to land animals (tetrapods). According to dating mechanisms, we know that land animals first appeared on earth about 370 million years ago. Until 2004, no good transitional species had been found. Neil Shubin[1] and his collaborators hypothesized that evolutionary theory predicts that if they search hard enough in rocks a little older than 370 million years of age, they will find fossils of species that have both fishlike and tetrapodlike characteristics. They knew that there were very few rock formations on earth of just the right age but identified one set in northern Canada. Beginning in 1999, they put together a crew that searched the rock formations for fossils that had the expected characteristics. Over a five-year period, the group went out to that area every summer and screened very carefully for fossils. Over the first four summers, they found nothing. Then toward the end of the summer of 2004, which they had decided would be the last year of the search project, they found a nearly complete specimen of a species that had exactly the predicted characteristics—a fossil which had certain fish and certain tetrapod characteristics. The results were consistent with their hypothesis. Most important for this discussion, though, is that this is just one hypothesis out of a huge number tested for various aspects of evolutionary theory. Not all have been confirmed. Some aspects of the original theory have proven false (or at least incomplete). As a result, for example, it is now clear that natural selection is not the only factor influencing the diversity of life. Darwin didn't even know about genes when he formulated his theory. We now know that a phenomenon known as genetic drift has also had an important influence on the diversity of life.

Here's the point. Science works through the process of constructing theories. A theory is tested through a whole set of hypotheses often by hundreds of scientists testing different aspects of the theory. Depending on the results of those tests, the theory may become modified as some aspects of it are shown not to agree with certain hypotheses. That is the situation with evolutionary theory. Thousands of scientists have tested thousands of hypotheses examining different aspects of evolutionary theory. This is done not so much to test the theory itself (it is considered to have been overwhelmingly confirmed) but to refine it and to understand the mechanisms at work at a deeper and deeper level. Although refinement has been going on for 150 years, no single aspect has ever been shown to be inconsistent with the broad principle of descent from a common ancestor. We'll examine a few more hypotheses later, but first I'd like to put this discussion back into the context of the discussion between Todd and me.

What concerns me about my Christian brother Todd is that even though he is very well informed about many of the massive number of hypotheses that have been tested and found to be consistent with evolutionary theory, he is unable to accept the conclusions shared by virtually every other graduate-trained evolutionary biologist in the world. While I don't question his scientific credentials, I'm not sure that what he's doing is science. Here is an example to illustrate why I say that. Let's say that you know someone who can't accept that the earth revolves around the sun. "Look in the sky," he says. "Clearly, the sun is moving. We see that movement every day from sunrise to sunset. We can even take time-lapse photographs of that movement. Has anyone actually seen the earth move?" With that in mind, the person goes on to develop a new model in which the sun moves and not the earth. Maybe he even proposes a cause for his proposed movement of the sun. He sets up some predictions about what would happen if his model is correct and sets out to test them, and he does this making use of his extensive knowledge of stars and galaxies. Is that person doing science?

Todd knows I feel this way, and it hurts me to say it because of my love and respect for him and his intentions—his beautiful intentions, actually. Todd knows that we almost read Scripture the same way. Given that we all know there is figurative language in other parts of Scripture, there have always been two ways of interpreting the creation story. Thousands of scientifically tested hypotheses are consistent with the notion that the biblical account was not meant to be taken literalistically. So it contains poetic elements that are meant to reveal everlasting truths about God as Creator, the cosmos as his creation, and the role that we humans are meant to occupy within it. Todd, and my many other friends who view this similarly, are holding out because they are convinced that their interpretation is correct. Most people don't know the depth of the evidence, but Todd does and he holds out anyway. This concerns me, because it implies that the analytical minds that God has given us cannot be trusted to lead us to anything that approximates truth. I can't buy that. As I see it, Todd's skepticism about this has broad ramifications for whether we can expect our minds to be reliable for knowing anything. Is this really consistent with the nature of the biblical God in whom we put our trust? I recognize that human minds can be distorted through sin. To believe thus is scriptural. But that's not the issue here. Both Todd and I love the Lord and seek to follow him more than anything in life, and both of us as biologists look at the data and see exactly the same thing—overwhelming support for evolutionary theory. One of us doesn't trust human reasoning despite overwhelming odds because of his conviction that God wouldn't speak in a poetic way about creation. But isn't this putting a sort of trust in the power of his own reasoning about this? Why should he trust his own reasoning about why God wouldn't use poetry to tell the creation story, but not his own reasoning about the solidity of the scientific data? Is there something more spiritual about believing that a particular interpretation (no poetry) is correct? I don't think so. Still, no matter what, Todd will likely continue to think he is right, and I will likely continue to think I am. In the meantime, we are together, arm in arm at the foot of the cross. Each doing our best to follow God's leading as we understand it. Each feeling a little mystified as to why God doesn't just reveal his truth to whichever of us is wrong.

Why does God leave us in this dilemma? I think that with that question I'm back to the question about that cherry leaf that never wiggled. God desires freedom for us. Mystery is not necessarily a bad thing. Perhaps a little misty fog and some ambiguity are essential and desirable parts of what it means to live in creation infused as it is with freedom. Without that, our existence might become almost robotic. A master who knows everything and reveals everything in textbook fashion leaves nothing for us to find out on our own. Paul, according to some translations of 1 Corinthians 13, calls this "seeing through a glass darkly." In the meantime, as we all peer through the fog, Paul reminds us of the danger of sounding like a noisy gong and a clanging cymbal. Instead we are to be instruments of harmonious love. We may not sound the same note, but we can ensure that our different notes sound forth through a single instrument of praise.

It's now time to return to the question of just how solid the evidence for evolution is. In my narrative, I gave one clear example of the evolutionary theory of common descent leading to a prediction that a certain rock formation of just the appropriate age found in Canada would, if searched carefully enough, provide fossils of animals intermediate between fish and four-legged land animals. My point is that evolutionary theory makes many predictions that can be tested. Here are a few more. For example, the theory predicts that if we can successfully date rocks, the fossils found therein will show a progression from single-cell organisms in the oldest rocks to increasingly complex organisms in rocks that are younger and younger. This is exactly what is found.

Scientists have developed radiometric dating, a method of fairly accurately determining the ages of various rocks and other objects based on the decay rate of radioactive isotopes. It sounds complex, and in a way it is, so I won't go into the details (though if you're really interested in the science behind it, I explain it in chapter 3 of my book, *Coming to Peace with Science*). Using radiometric dating, scientists have determined that the earth is anywhere from 4.3 billion to 4.6 billion years old. And this age is determined not by a single radiometric test but by several. There are forty different tests using isotopes to determine the age of minerals, and all arrive at the same conclusion, which is that the earth is very old. Frequently there are ways of cross-checking a calculated age with one set of isotopes, using a different set of isotopes with different decay rates. When this is done, there is a clear progression in the types of fossils found in the rocks. Rocks that are greater than one billion years old have never revealed a fossil of a multicellular plant or animal, or any parts thereof. In rocks that are less than one billion years or so old, we sometimes see signs of multicellular organisms in the fossil record. To begin with, though, they are very simple organisms. Beginning around 543 million years of age, the rocks begin to contain most of the major animal phyla (groups) that are represented today. They are small, fairly simple, and do not contain any species that we would find in more recent rocks (say, 250 million years or younger). But there is a progression as we move through time to examine rocks that are younger and younger. Fish first appear in rocks of about 500 million years. No other vertebrates are found, though, only fish in rocks of that age. Amphibians appear beginning in rocks of about 370 million years and they are then found in samples up to the present age. Reptiles appear a little later (about 320 million years) and mammals (230 million years) a little later still. Here is the point I wish to make. Science allows us to test the hypothesis that if evolution is correct, there would be a progression of fossils that is correlated with the age of the rocks that contain them. The hypothesis has been tested over and over again—hundreds of times—and there are no known cases where the dated rocks contain fossils that are inconsistent with the described pattern.

What about humans? The first primates are not found in the fossil record until rocks dated at 55 million years ago. Since humans are primates, it follows that no humanlike ("hominin" is the scientific term) fossils have ever been in rock formations older than this. In actuality, geologists have scoured the earth's surface, and although thousands of hominin fossils have now been found, none are found in rocks older than about five million years. This means that hominin fossils are found only in about 0.1 percent of the age-range of dated rock formations. Fossils of lots of other organisms are found in formations of various ages, but no hominins until we come to formations that are relatively young.

Now we come to the next important observation: rock formations of between two million and five million years of age contain no hominin fossils the world over, except on one continent—Africa. Indeed, no hominin fossils have ever been found in North or South America that are older than about eighteen thousand years. Rock formations of the appropriate ages are present, of course, but they contain no hominin fossils. In Asia, hominin fossils are found beginning at about 1.8 million years and in Europe about one million years. This regional localization is consistent with the hypothesis that hominins were created through a single evolutionary lineage in one area of the world—Africa. This is what Darwin predicted 150 years ago based upon the fact that the species that most closely resemble humans are found there. Since they do eventually make their appearance in Asia and then Europe, the findings suggest that a group migrated out of Africa (perhaps over many generations) into Asia a little less than two million years ago, and that some of their descendants in turn eventually made it into Europe. The oceans presented a barrier, of course, to arrival in North and South America, hence the rock formations in the western hemisphere show no hominin presence until the last 0.5 percent of hominin existence.[2]

Todd, of course, knows this data well, and he thinks, in essence, that the various hominin species were unique instantaneous creations that subsequently went extinct. Like Todd, I think their existence is a result of the process by which God chose to create humankind. I recognize, though, that what Todd proposes is a valid possibility were it not for the vast amount of data that has been accumulating in my discipline of genetics. I'll never forget the exhilaration I felt when I was first introduced to genetics in college. I've written elsewhere that "the living process of a single cell, and the unfolding and coordination of the plan for a developing embryo, were like a magnificent symphony, and I felt that I would never be able to find a greater intellectual joy than I would by spending the rest of my life studying its orchestration."[3] The primary focus of my career in higher education has been genetics, and the more I studied and learned, the more I became convinced that all that has happened is wonderfully consistent with theism. Its beauty and process are exactly what we would expect if a loving God, whom we know from revelation (the Bible) and personal experience, works through time to bring about his purposes. God's initial design and God's providential oversight work through life's processes to bring about creation of new life forms.

For example, we can observe genetic elements. It is also through genetics that we learn with near certainty that even humans were created through the evolutionary process. I want to explain ever so briefly why I think this is so. Here's one example of the many sorts of examples that I could choose. There are hundreds of thousands of small pieces of DNA that move ever so slowly from one location to another in chromosomes, the long strings of DNA molecules where genes reside. On average, any given genetic element will move ("jump") into a new location at an average rate of less than one jump per 500,000 generations. (We can determine their approximate rate of jumping because there are so many of these genetic elements.) So even though one specific element hardly ever jumps, since there are so many of them, we can occasionally follow some specific moves and then extrapolate to measure the rate of movement in general. Here's the point. In chimpanzees and humans, many of the genetic elements are in the *exact* same location. (Functionally, it has been shown that there is no specific reason that they need to be in the same location.) This is consistent with the hypothesis that chimpanzees and humans descend from a common ancestral species that existed about five or six million years ago and that given how slowly the genetic elements jump to a new location, most are still in the same location in that common ancestor. If one compares the position of these jumping elements in orangutans, there is a higher percentage that don't occupy the same position in the chromosomes. This is consistent with the hypothesis that orangutans and humans share a common ancestral species (many of the elements are still in *exactly* the same location), but one that existed deeper in the past. Gibbons are another primate, and they are even more distantly related to humans than orangutans as judged by comparing various anatomical characteristics. If we examine the distribution of the jumping genetic elements in gibbons, many are still in the exact same positions as in humans, but a higher percentage have shifted. This is consistent with the hypothesis that gibbons and humans descend from a common ancestral species even deeper in the past, allowing even greater time for elements to jump. Again, since there is no functional reason for them to be in *exactly* the same position, the data implies that the shared positioning is a reflection of the chromosomes being passed successively through sperm and eggs for hundreds of thousands of generations in each of the two lineages.[4]

As a scientist who is also a Christian, I see three possible responses to the overwhelming evidence for evolution. A person might agree that the earth is very old and that life has evolved over millions of years and might therefore conclude that the biblical account of creation is wrong. Almost all evolutionary biologists have done just that and, in the process, have rejected the Christian faith altogether. Second, a person might also accept the evidence but claim that it still isn't enough to convince one that the earth is very old and that life has evolved over time. That's what Todd and other YECs have done, which is why the scientific community does not take young-earth creationists or in some cases even their Christian faith seriously. Or third, one can try to find a way to reconcile the evidence for evolution with the biblical account of creation.

Initially, as I wrote earlier, I could not reconcile the science that I was studying with the literal interpretation of Genesis 1, and ultimately, for a while I fell away from my Christian faith. To be fair, as I mentioned, it wasn't just this issue of origins that led me to abandon my faith. As a budding geneticist in the rarified air of the academy, I got caught up not only in my career but also in a lifestyle that at the time seemed more sophisticated and exciting than life as an evangelical Christian.

I don't take lightly Todd's concern, then, that introducing young Christian college students to evolution and encouraging them to evaluate it objectively could open the door for them to question everything about their faith and eventually leave it. I'll never forget Rachael,[5] a brilliant young woman who came into our Christian college on an almost full-tuition scholarship. She had come from a fundamentalist church and knew all of the arguments for a young-earth, no-evolution perspective that are found in the creationist books and was a strong supporter. She was a wonderful Christian, a spiritual leader on our campus for her entire four years there. Rachael knew I thought much differently than her about evolution, and listened closely as I explained the fundamentals of mainstream evolutionary science in the various courses in which she was consistently one of my best students. She explained the mainstream view well on her essay exams, even though both of us knew that she did not hold to those views. The two of us connected well, perhaps in no small part because she knew my story; she knew how close I had been to deciding that there would be no place for someone like me and my family in evangelical Christianity. So we were good friends, even though we thought differently about evolution. About ten years later, I renewed my contact with Rachael. She was now a successful neurosurgeon with her own practice. We corresponded a little about my work with BioLogos and I proceeded to communicate about some faith matters in much the same way as Rachael and I had done during her student days. However, she quickly let me know that she had spent some time with the New Atheist literature since leaving our Christian college and that Christianity no longer worked for her. She was now an atheist. The secular university environment, where evolution was taken for granted by all of her colleagues, together with the books that she'd read had shown her that her earlier thoughts about a young earth and no evolution did not hold up to careful scrutiny. My view of the compatibility of the Christian faith and evolution seemed to be a compromise, and she knew of no other way to retain a meaningful faith. Her upbringing in Christianity was so closely tied to a tightly constructed fundamentalism with no room for mystery that when the prescription did not work, it left only one choice as she saw it: a whole different brand of fundamentalism. Here too there was no mystery, just a tightly constructed set of facts grounded in the absence of God and the algorithm of natural selection alone. Her past became one big fairy tale, and to this point she had been unable to put her once vibrant faith in God back together again.

Like Todd, and like Rachael originally thought, I believe Genesis 1. Further, I believe there is no message on earth more important than the creation story, when told in its completeness, centered in Christ and bathed in mystery. It is how John begins both his gospel and his epistles:

> In the beginning was the Word. . . . All things came into being through him, and without him not one thing came into being. (John 1:1, 3 NRSV)

> We declare to you what was from the beginning . . .

that God is light and in him there is no darkness at all.
(1 John 1:1, 5 NRSV)

The introduction of the letter to the Hebrews (1:10 NRSV) includes the following:

In the beginning, Lord, you founded the earth, and the heavens are the work of your hands.

And Paul lays it out so beautifully in the introduction of his letter to the church at Colossae (Col. 1:16 NRSV):

In him all things in heaven and on earth were created, things visible and invisible, whether thrones or dominions or rulers or powers—all things have been created through him and for him.

And of course, we have many beautiful poetic descriptions of creation in Psalms (8, 19, and 104, for example) and elsewhere in the Old Testament.

Unlike Todd, I do not believe that the description of how God created the earth and life in Genesis 1–3 should be taken literally, as in a newspaper account. The purpose of the account in all of its richness was to speak into the culture of the hearers, putting the creation story into a framework that addressed the questions of the Hebrew people in contrast to the creation narratives of their bar-baric neighbors. When the Bible says "God created," it did so in a form and using language that could be understood by people who lived three thousand years or so ago. It's a language that has been amazingly coherent through the ages, speaking just as powerfully to us today as it did to our ancestors. However, the biblical story was not meant to be a scientific account of precisely how God did it. If God had gone into that in detail to a culture of three thou-sand years ago, it wouldn't have made any sense to them, and they never would have gotten the message, which is not only that God created but also that he wants to enter into a relationship with us. It doesn't in any way concern me that the details are not in the Bible but rather that we have this picture that God designed and created the pro-cess of evolution and that the process continues because of God's ongoing presence. If God hadn't been present in the first place, and hadn't been present and active ever since, nothing would exist that does exist.

Todd and other young-earth creationists cannot bring themselves to make what I consider to be a very small shift in the way they read the early chapters of Genesis. Obviously, Todd would not agree that this is such a small shift but would say that it leads to abandoning the truth and trustworthiness of the Bible in much the same way that Rachael resolved her dilemma. But when I say that I do not think the Bible was meant to be a scientific text-book explaining in detail exactly how God created, I am in no way denying the truth that God created the heavens and the earth. Nor is this way of reading Genesis necessarily a slippery slope into liberal theology. Many respected early Christian thinkers embraced the same general view that while the Bible is God's revealed Word to his people, it is not a science book. In the fourth century, Augustine warned against claiming that the Bible holds scientific truths, because as science changed, people would lose their trust in the Bible. John Calvin did not specifically address creationism because it was not a pressing issue in his day, but he saw the purpose of Scripture to be oriented more theologically than scientifically. To him, the primary purpose of the Bible is to lead us to a knowledge of Jesus. He once wrote that the Bible "was never intended to provide us with an infallible repository of astronomical and medical information."[6] The great reformer John Wesley held a similar view, asserting that Genesis 1 was written not to satisfy our curiosity about, for example, the stars but to lead us to God.

I know that Todd and other YECs believe that those of us who do not read Genesis 1 literally are treading dangerous ground. I not only disagree but consider this issue to be a question about the truthfulness of the Christian faith itself. We ought not to tangentially attach to the Christian faith something that is as untrue as the views of creation held by young-earth creationists. I am certain that if the Lord tarries, it will become widely known that evolution was God's way of creation. As the church is able to accept this over time, I think it will lead to a richer understanding of God—the ultimate goal of every Christian. If this is God's way of creating all that exists, it will enrich us all theologically, and all of Christ's followers will well up with even richer and more meaningful praise. God's ways are not our ways, and too often I think we tend to put God into our humanly constructed boxes. Still, God has given us the amazing power to reason at a level infinitely greater than that of any other creature in his creation. That gift really does enable us to see him more clearly, to love him more deeply, and to grow in our understanding of his creative handiwork so that we might enjoy his creation and become a celebration of praise that lasts forever and ever.

I am not an evolutionary creationist because I want to fit in with the rest of the scientific world. Rather, I believe that this process is an accurate description of how God created because of the overwhelming evidence. Science is revealing the details of God's activity, and those who close their minds to this revelation are missing the opportunity to see more clearly the work of the God we love so much.

———————— **For Study and Reflection** ————————

1. If you are a young-earth creationist, describe your thoughts and feelings as you read this chapter, especially the evidence for evolution that Darrel shared.

2. If you accept the theory of evolution, why do you think it is so difficult for people like Todd to acknowledge that God used the evolutionary process to create the heavens and the earth?

3. Many creationists have criticized Todd for agreeing that much of the evidence that Darrel cites is true. How do you think creationists should respond to the preponderance of evidence for evolution?

4. As recently as twenty-five years ago, most evangelical Christians were young-earth creationists. Today, the percentage of evangelical Christians who accept evolution has grown significantly. Why do you think this has happened?

5. What can the church and its Christian colleges and universities do to support students like Rachael who imply that accepting evolution led them to abandon their faith?

6. What qualities about Darrel's approach to science do you admire? What qualities do you find less admirable?

CHAPTER 10

WHAT ABOUT THE WHALES?

Todd Charles Wood

Even though I don't think it's entirely correct, evolution is a fascinating subject. It became my main area of study in graduate school. Specifically, I studied evolutionary biochemistry, which is all about how the chemistry of living things makes them the way they are. Honestly, it was challenging and remarkable and beautiful. There were many times as I sat in class or worked on my own research that I thought, "Wow! This stuff is really persuasive. I can see why people think evolution is true." Sometimes I tried to think how a creationist might explain the things I studied, but like I said before, this was way beyond the standard creationist ideas I was familiar with. Obviously, something new was needed in creationism.

Some of my creationist colleagues don't like it when

I say things like that. There's a long tradition in creationism, stretching back to the first critics of Darwin himself, of claiming that evolutionary theory is a scientific failure or not even scientific at all. It's not fashionable to claim otherwise, that's for sure. Other creationists just find what I say about evolution discouraging, either personally or to others. They worry that I'll drive students right out of Christianity and into the jaws of evolutionists waiting to gobble them up. I think there's far more danger in not owning up to reality. It's not like students won't find out about the evidence for evolution, and I'd rather they hear it from me than from someone intent on destroying their faith.

On the other hand, I know that Darrel and other Christian evolutionists think I should just accept the preponderance of evidence that suggests that human beings, like all other life on this planet, evolved. There's no reason to reinterpret all of science, since we can tweak our theology just a little bit and everything fits. Why bother with some other explanation when we already know the "right" answer? And why bother causing so much unnecessary anxiety and embarrassment to the church?

Except, if you dig a little deeper—if you refuse to accept something just because everyone else does—you might find something new, and that's what I love about being a scientist. As a Christian and a scientist, I have a choice to make. I can play the game of methodological naturalism and try to hold my science away from my faith and just go with the crowd. Or I can live a life of true integration, with all the uncertainty that brings. I don't always know how the Bible and scientific data fit together, but I am confident that the answers are out there. If I work hard enough, I might even find a few.

For example, Darrel and other evolutionists point to fossils of a whalelike creature with hind legs that seem to indicate that whales evolved from land creatures. Over the past twenty years or so, there have been many discoveries of fossils with telltale characteristics of modern whales and with hind legs of various degrees of development. Animals like *Pakicetus* appear to have had four full legs, but other fossil creatures like *Dorudon* or *Basilosaurus* had much smaller hind legs. Most whales today have small bones where their hips would be. So it seems pretty persuasive to put these fossils in a series that shows the gradual evolution of modern whales from four-legged ancestors.[1]

Yet when I read Genesis, it tells me that God created the great sea creatures on the fifth day. That's not really consistent with this model of whale evolution, or at least it doesn't *seem* to be. So I wonder, maybe there are other ways of thinking about these creatures? How can I test the evolution of whales? That turns out to be really difficult because all of modern science is built on the concepts of evolution. How can I test what is taken as self-evident?

For me, that's where the fun begins. The challenge that I've run into is that I can't really test evolution directly. Instead, I like to look for what I call discontinuity. In simple terms, discontinuities are like gaps in the fossil record, but discontinuity is discovered using fancy math called cluster analysis.[2] For the whales and whale fossils, I want to know whether that group of creatures forms an unbroken sequence from four-legged ancestor to modern whale. Using the data collected by evolutionary biologists, I discovered that it doesn't. The fossil whales with hind legs are distinct from modern whales.[3] There's a discontinuity between modern whales and fossil four-legged "whales." That's clearly not enough to unravel evolutionary theory (at any level, really), but it raises an interesting question: How widespread is this discontinuity? If I look at some other examples of evolution, will I find the same thing?

The fossil horse series is another famous example of evolution, showing what appears to be a gradual change from a small, dog-sized horse called *Hyracotherium* to the modern donkeys, zebras, and Clydesdales. I've evaluated horses with the same methods I used on the whales. To my surprise, I did not find discontinuity. Instead, I found what appeared to be a nice, unbroken series from

Hyracotherium to living horses. They're all horses, of course (of course), but there's no evidence of clusters or gaps.[4]

The average Christian doesn't care much about whales or horses, so this research might seem a little pointless. But I can apply the same techniques to the fossil record of humans and apes, which I think is far more interesting. The fossils are called "hominins," and there are lots of them. Many have traits that are today found only in apes or only in humans. For example, the famous Lucy fossil, *Australopithecus afarensis*, had a flat face, a protruding muzzle, and a small brain like today's apes. Lucy also had knees and hips for walking upright on two legs, like modern people. Do these hominin fossils show an unbroken sequence from nonhuman to human? Or are there distinct groups of humans and apes?

Once again, I've been amazed by what I've uncovered. First and most important, there are distinct clusters of humans and apes just like there are clusters of different sorts of whales. There is not an unbroken sequence of fossils connecting humans to nonhuman animals. On the other hand, the group that contains us modern people is a lot bigger than I expected, with some forms that don't look a lot like us. That's more like what I found with the horses, where tiny *Hyracotherium* ends up in the same group with modern horses.[5]

So what does any of this mean? I think it's easier to tell you what it doesn't mean. It doesn't mean that evolution has been disproved. Evolution is a lot bigger than just gradual transitions from one form to another. These clusters of whales and hominins don't even answer all of the questions about whales and hominins! Finding discontinuity also doesn't prove creation or the flood. I'm not even sure what sort of evidence would do that.

If it doesn't prove anything, why bother with this discontinuity stuff? If you can't make a solid conclusion, what's the point? That's a reasonable question, and I think it reveals one of the most important problems with the creation-evolution debate: Everyone wants it all solved *right now*. If something isn't conclusive, it isn't valuable. But that's not how life works. We all need to stop and take a deep breath and rediscover our ignorance. The idea that we can conclusively disprove evolution is a fantasy. So is the idea that the Bible and theology "easily" accommodate evolution. These are hard problems, and it's going to take time to sort through them. Answers aren't always going to be satisfying. Just coming up with good questions that we *can* answer is hard enough.

Discontinuity excites me, though, because of what I've discovered. I've been doing this sort of work for nearly twenty years now, and I've tested hundreds of different groups.[6] More often than not, I find discontinuity.

I'm starting to get a good idea of the landscape of living things without evolution telling me what I'm supposed to see. It may not solve all of our problems, but it's one step in a direction I think all Christians need to think seriously about.

Discontinuity also excites me because discontinuity is science. I gather data. I evaluate it. I draw conclusions. I think about the next step in my research project. It's science. It's not theology or apologetics. I'm not out to prove things. I want to learn and discover more about God's creation. So those people who tell me science can be done only one way are just not right. We really can think more carefully about science, and I think we Christians ought to support those efforts.

Ultimately creation studies like mine act like road signs. Back before smart phones and GPS, I relied on paper maps and road signs to guide me to my destination. I used the map to set out the general plan of where I wanted to go, but I needed road signs to tell me I was on the right track. Every successful and fruitful creation study that I encounter is just like that: it tells me I'm on the right track. Even when I don't know all of the answers to all of the scientific puzzles, I keep looking at the world with creationist glasses, and it keeps making sense.

Another signpost comes from studying the flood. As a creationist, I think that the flood really happened and that it really covered the entire globe. Once again, though, "proving" that is challenging, but lots of creationists have examined pieces of the flood, and they make sense.

A recent example of flood geology research comes from the work of John Whitmore, a geology professor at Cedarville University. For about fifteen years, John has been studying a layer of sandstone near the top ridge of the Grand Canyon known as the Coconino Sandstone. Most geologists believe this layer of sandstone was formed by windblown sand, meaning it was formed in a desert environment. But John and his students found lots of evidence that the Coconino was formed underwater.[7]

John presented his findings at several conferences of the Geological Society of America.[8] Naturally, he's had a difficult time getting the full papers published, because they challenge the conventional wisdom of most geologists. Once again, his research doesn't prove the biblical account of a global flood, but it's fascinating that these kinds of things keep happening. If we creationists were barking up the wrong tree and holding on to a perfectly ludicrous model (which is what many evolutionists think we're doing), I would think we wouldn't get *anywhere* when we start doing creation research. But looking at things differently is a perfectly scientific thing to do, and that's what John Whitmore did when he began poking around in the Coconino Sandstone. Nearly every other geologist thought these were sand dunes, but he came up with a different—and better—way of looking at this sandstone. We don't fully understand how the Coconino fits into the larger model of the global flood, but John's discoveries encourage people like me to keep looking at the world with an open mind. I find this happening over and over again. When creationists take the conventional model, turn it on its head, look at the data again, things start making sense from a creationist viewpoint. I can't help but think it's probably because we're on the right track.

Plenty of people in Darrel's camp still think what I'm doing is unnecessary. For them, the science is settled. There's no need to bother with reimagining any of it, but science for me is immensely fuzzy and uncertain. Nothing is ever settled.

When I was in graduate school, I worked for a while on something called protein crystallography, which tells us about the molecular structure of proteins. In the simplest of terms, this involves creating crystals of the proteins, shooting X-rays at them, and then using incredibly complicated math to turn the results into something that resembles a chemical structure. I saw from these experiments just how much uncertainty there was. Sometimes the proteins weren't perfectly uniform in their crystal, so the crystals weren't very good. Sometimes there were technical limitations with the X-rays and how the X-ray results were collected. All of these led to protein structures that were unavoidably uncertain. Despite that uncertainty, I also observed the pragmatism of science that says that the theory that explains the most information is the one we'll accept, even if it's not perfect. Until we have a better model, we'll go with what we have. I see something similar happening with origins. Yes, evolution seems to explain a lot about how we ended up with our modern diversity of species. But so much remains fuzzy and uncertain. Science is never settled. There's always room for more research.

For me, this quest to find better answers is not depressing or anxiety-producing, even if I have more questions than answers. It's exciting. It's my faith. There is a God out there who not only created this beautiful world but gave us his Son, Jesus, who loves me and died for my sins. It is a privilege to get out of bed every morning to see what new things God has for me. It's absolutely thrilling to observe the world around me and ask, "What's really going on here?" What new stars have been discovered? What new fossils are out there? What new discoveries are waiting for us? It's not disappointing. It's one of the greatest joys of life. I'm looking at God's creation, and ultimately that leads me back to him, and that's well worth the quest.

———————— **For Study and Reflection** ————————

1. Why would someone who is so committed to a young-earth creationist view pursue an advanced degree in evolutionary science? Can you think of other examples of someone studying a topic that he is convinced is false or inaccurate?

2. Todd warns against accepting something just because everyone else does. Can you think of other areas where Christians appear to have accepted something because it is popular? What are the advantages and disadvantages of such acceptance?

3. Todd suggests that his approach to evolutionary evidence comes partly from looking at that evidence with an open mind. How can having an open mind be helpful, and how can it cause problems? In your experience, what factors determine whether you are going to be open to a new idea?

4. Creation scientists like Todd receive little financial support, which, they believe, limits their ability to compete at the research level with the more widely accepted evolutionary scientists. As a Christian, regardless of your views on origins, do you think creation scientists should receive more substantial funding for their work? Why or why not?

5. What qualities about Todd's approach to science do you admire? What qualities do you find less admirable?

BEYOND DISAGREEMENT

Rob Barrett, The Colossian Forum

We seem to be stuck. This story doesn't seem to be ending right. I suppose, after those last two chapters, folks in Todd's camp will be cheering their champion and shaking their heads at Darrel. And vice versa. Where's the happy ending where we figure out "The Right Answer" and all end up in cheerful agreement? If we do this right and treat each other kindly, doesn't God owe it to us to make the answers clear? Where's the resolution to the debate?

That's just not how it seems to work, at least so far.

We are stuck in a messy place. I once asked our two scientists if they saw each other as friends or enemies. I was confident, after all of our time together, that they would agree that they were friends. Todd disappointed me when he answered, "Not just enemies. Mortal enemies." I looked pleadingly to gentle Darrel for the correction Todd needed. He failed me too: "Yes, Todd's right." My little plan continued to backfire as they decided to write a couple of blog posts talking about their enmity. (You can read their exchange on Todd's blog *toddcwood.blogspot.com*. Todd's piece is titled "I'd Rather NOT Be Swallowed by a Giant Fish," and Darrel's response, also on Todd's blog, is "Don't Be Like Jonah.")

As they wrote in their opening chapters, both Darrel and Todd think that the other's error is a dangerous one. People get hurt when we get this wrong. But here's the thing. Getting our position right about origins is important, but it's not the most important thing. It's like what Paul writes: "If I . . . can fathom all mysteries and all knowledge . . . but do not have love, I am nothing" (1 Cor. 13:2). If I can figure out all of the intricacies of faith and science, but have not love, "I am only a resounding gong or a clanging cymbal" (v. 1). It's more important to get love, real Jesus-style love, right than getting the answers to this problem right.

Darrel and Todd would both quickly jump in at this point to say, "But don't think origins isn't important!" I totally agree. What these two Christian men understand well is that origins is important because it's one part of learning to love God and our neighbors well. Everything is interconnected. Getting origins right isn't the most important thing, but our missteps about origins might lead to getting even more important things wrong.

Saint Augustine described it well some sixteen hundred years ago in his book *On Christian Doctrine*. What he wrote about interpreting the Bible also applies to interpreting science. Augustine noted that getting to the wrong answer means you've gone astray. He goes on, "Nevertheless . . . if his mistaken interpretation tends to build up love, which is the end of the commandment, he goes astray in much the same way as a man who by mistake quits the high road, but yet reaches through fields the same place."[1] If you get things wrong in such a way that you end up doing what God wanted you to do anyway, then it's not so bad. Still, Augustine argued, it's best to get things right. If you can help someone who is making a mistake, you should do so. He continues, "He is to be corrected, however, and to be shown how much better it is not to quit the straight road, lest, if he get into a habit of going astray, he may sometimes take cross roads, or even go in the wrong direction altogether."[2]

Both Darrel and Todd have this sense about the other. Even if the other is wrong, they seem to be doing well for right now. Still, straying from the truth here might lead to straying further and making critical mistakes. As these two struggle through their serious disagreement, their focus remains on helping the other stay on the straight and narrow path.

As you read their final chapters, what can you take away from their experience that might help you contend for the truth in a way that honors God and helps those with whom you disagree?

CHAPTER 11

IS DARREL A HERETIC?

Todd Charles Wood

What Darrel and I have tried to do isn't easy. That should never be an excuse for behavior toward fellow believers that does not reflect the love of Christ. But we're human. We fail. And this topic is incredibly important to me. It really is about a lot more than how God created the earth. It's about whether we can trust the clarity of the Bible, where we learn about God and his plan for salvation, and that's pretty important.

As Darrel and I have talked through some difficult questions, I always bring up "Aunt Myrtle" (not really my aunt). She reads her Bible in English and believes that God speaks to her through that Bible. She has come to know Jesus in those pages. She can see his life and the things that are important to him and, therefore, the things that should be important to her as well. At times, just when she needs it, God's Word speaks to her in a way that is soothing or inspiring; it miraculously gives her just what she needs to make it through her day. She might not understand everything she reads, but on the big stuff that really matters, it all seems pretty clear to her. She reads the Gospels and learns that God sent Jesus into the world so that she could experience the free gift of salvation. She reads the epistles, and their instructions on how to live a godly life make sense. Jeremiah, Amos, Habakkuk—she's not real sure what's going on there, but that very first chapter in the very first book of the Bible? The one that she first heard in Sunday school? It's as clear to her as it is beautiful.

What people like Darrel need to understand is that when you tell people like Aunt Myrtle that the story really doesn't mean what it says, it's devastating to them. That is a catastrophically shocking moment. It's frightening to be confronted with the idea that it didn't really happen the way you read it in plain, simple English. If Aunt Myrtle takes that seriously, she feels duped. She thought she understood the Bible, but now she's not so sure. And then she begins to think, "What else haven't I understood? What else have I gotten wrong?" It's terrifying, especially when the guy telling you that you were wrong about the Bible is a Christian.

The easy way out for Aunt Myrtle is to reject what Darrel is saying. Aunt Myrtle might think that Darrel can't possibly be right, so he must not really be a Christian! Why do so many in the young-earth creationist movement feel so strongly about what's happening? It's because from their perspective, Darrel is challenging the foundation of Christian faith. They react just like Aunt Myrtle. If we can't understand what Genesis says, then how can we be sure we understand any of the other clear passages of Scripture? Many conservative evangelical Christians in thousands of churches across North America believe just like Aunt Myrtle, and they send money to the big creationist organizations that support their beliefs. And, of course, Darrel helped start an organization which basically does the same thing (even though BioLogos thought they might provide a resolution to the conflict). This conflict is where we are today, and part of the reason is that Christian evolutionists wield their arguments recklessly and endanger the faith of thousands of believers just like Aunt Myrtle.

Aunt Myrtle could react another way to Darrel and company, but she would probably never consider it for herself. Her children or grandchildren are another story, though. They could say, "If the Bible really doesn't mean what it says, then I've been lied to. I don't want to be a Christian anymore." It might not happen as quickly and intentionally as that, but many young people seem quite willing to drop the faith of their parents if they decide that the Bible doesn't really mean what they thought it meant.

There was a time when I was suspicious of the faith of people like Darrel. I would tell my students that there are evolutionists who claim to be Christians, and that was carefully chosen wording. I never wanted to give the impression that what Darrel believes is a real option for Christians, but I didn't want openly to judge them as unchristian. If people like Darrel really are Christians, they are most certainly sinful ones.

This little experiment of engaging with Darrel over the long haul has caused me to do some soul-searching. I've discovered that Darrel is very concerned about Aunt Myrtle. Darrel thinks what *I* am doing is setting up the Aunt Myrtles of the church to become disillusioned. *I* am reinforcing Aunt Myrtle's false understanding of the Bible. Though he might never use these words, *I'm* the heretic because I'm misleading Christians. I'm promoting something that's not true.

I suppose that should be obvious, right? Of course, he thinks he's right and I'm wrong. There wouldn't be a conflict if he didn't. But it goes beyond that. Sitting with Darrel, listening to his frustrations with creationists, and, even more important, praying with him leads to a much more visceral unveiling. He's worried about the *very same things I am.* If it weren't for evolution, I'd look at him and find myself looking right back.

That's a hard thing to discover. My enemy is just like me. Even worse, sometimes in our disagreement, he has a point. I've been frustrated too, seeing fellow creationists push theories or speculations as if they were settled truths. Disillusionment and mistaken faith can be just as devastating to Aunt Myrtle as unnecessary threats to her good faith in Christ and the Bible. God help us all.

Getting to know Darrel hasn't been easy. It still isn't. I'm not sure where these conversations will take us. We haven't solved anything about creation, if that was even the goal. But I understand why evolution is so important to him, and it's not because he wants to fit in. He accepts evolution because he believes it's true, and he has come to terms with his faith. He's found a way to live with evolution and the Bible. I still think he's wrong and dangerous, but there's more at stake here than our rightness and wrongness.

I have discovered in our times together a fulfillment of Christ's promise that when two or more are gathered together, he is there. Even now after getting to know Darrel and even growing to like him, there is still a part of me that wants to refuse every invitation to meet with him. I have to argue with that part of me every time, and every time I win that argument when I remember that when Darrel and I are together, Jesus is there. God is at work. I still have no idea what God wants to do with the two of us, but I want to find out. So, invitations come, and I go because I can't wait to find out what happens next!

Sometimes I talk to people who want to know exactly what's going on when Darrel and I get together. What's the big deal? As I've said, we haven't solved anything, but we still manage to get along. Are we just sitting around singing "Kumbaya"? No, that's not it either. This isn't some silly exercise in ignoring differences for the sake of false unity. This is different.

The book of Romans tells us that the Holy Spirit prays for us with groans that cannot be uttered. That's really the best way I can describe what happens. Sometimes the Spirit shows me things about Darrel that I really didn't understand. Sometimes the Spirit shows me things about myself that I don't particularly like. Sometimes we pray together or mourn together or rejoice together. Sometimes we're just together. It doesn't make sense, but once you've experienced it, it doesn't need to make sense. It just needs to be.

I'm not sure I've learned any lessons from my time with Darrel, but I have discovered something that I think is really important. Christians rarely disagree *together*, and that's hurting the church just as much as the disagreement itself. When we hear ideas that seem so threatening to our faith, it's easy for us to retreat. We Protestants especially imagine ourselves as little Martin Luthers posting the ninety-five theses all over again. We go back to the familiar comforts of friends and family, and we are reassured that "those people" must be evil. And the body of Christ is divided.

The night before Jesus died on the cross, he prayed for me in the garden of Gethsemane. He prayed for those who would believe because of the teaching of the apostles, and that's me. (You too, I hope.) At that critical moment, as the weight of the world's sin was placed on his back, as my sin was placed on his back, Jesus prayed for me and all the rest of us who believe in him. He prayed that we would be one, even as he and the Father are one.

Every time I want to retreat from Darrel, every time I want to take comfort from my simplistic stereotypes, I'm reminded of the time Jesus prayed for me. And every time Darrel and I meet (in spite of myself), I'm reminded how important Jesus' prayer really is. Jesus could have prayed for correct teaching and doctrine, which are important. Jesus could have prayed that false doctrine would be rooted out of the church, which is also important. Instead, Jesus prayed that we would stick together. When Darrel and I gather in Jesus' name, I find that the urgency of our disagreements dims ever so slightly as we struggle through hard questions with Jesus at our sides.

I have to confess that I've been pretty terrible at Christian unity. Some might even think I'm a hypocrite with what I'm writing. I'd guess that many of my fellow young-age creationists would describe me as divisive. As I write this, I imagine some whom I've offended are verbally scoffing at me as they read these words. I have not practiced forbearance or kindness in the past toward those who disagree with me. I still struggle every time I read or hear a fellow Christian declare with unflagging confidence that some nonsense is true and solves the whole creation-evolution debate.

And I'm sorry. I want my experience with Darrel to be my experience every time a fellow believer and I disagree about creation. I don't want to be that obnoxious jerk anymore. I don't know if that's realistic, but I know that destructive conflict requires two people. I don't have to be the second one. I don't have to stoke the fires of culture war. I want to spread the good news of the gospel: in the midst of human brokenness, Jesus offers salvation. As I talk with Darrel about our deepest disagreements, I've experienced that gospel for myself. It's intoxicating.

I'm not very good at it, but I want this unity in Christ to become the pattern of my life. I hope you'll join me.

——————— **For Study and Reflection** ———————

1. Earlier in their relationship, Todd believed Darrel accepted evolution because he wanted to fit in. Now Todd accepts that Darrel wasn't trying to fit in but simply believes evolution is true. Why do you think he changed his view of Darrel?

2. Regarding "Aunt Myrtle," who represents the average layperson in conservative churches, who is more guilty of misleading her, Todd or Darrel? Why?

3. Todd accepts much of the evidence for evolution yet remains convinced that the Genesis account of creation is literally true. What do you admire about his position? What concerns you about his position?

4. To most in the scientific community, people who believe in creation are fools. Do you think Todd's quest as a scientist to search for evidence to support biblical creationism gives legitimacy to creationism, or is he just wasting his time? Explain.

5. Todd has paid a huge price for his particular approach to creationism in that both creationists and evolutionists dismiss his work. What does this say about both the creationists and the scientific community—specifically Christian evolutionists?

CHAPTER 12

IS TODD A FOOL?

Darrel R. Falk

It's safe to say that neither Todd nor I is especially comfortable using words like "fool" and "heretic." In referring to Todd, I would be much more inclined to use terms like "intellectually brilliant" and "saintly." We hope you understand that fool and heretic are not words that we would use, but unfortunately others we know have used these terms to describe members of our respective communities. There is no room for this attitude within the Christian community. We're all on a journey following the same Lord, even though it sometimes seems that we are being led in such different directions.

I have met many scientifically and mathematically trained individuals who are young-earth creationists. They are the very antithesis of foolish. It is their love for the things of God that leads them to the position they hold. They believe that God, being the source of all reality, would not communicate in opaque or downright misleading ways in matters as important as how creation occurred. They also believe that there is a danger that allowing for figurative language on this issue will open the floodgates for reinterpreting other passages in Scripture, including those having to do with the miracles of Jesus and his physical resurrection. They have valid reasons for this concern. Liberal Christianity in the early part of the twentieth century did indeed go down this slope, and its acceptance of evolution played at least some role in initiating the slide.

Furthermore, most of the young-earth-creation proponents, unlike Todd with his graduate training in evolutionary biochemistry, are under the impression that there are considerable weaknesses in the evidence for evolution. They are trusting their experts, who for the most part are not really experts with doctoral-level training in evolutionary biology. But whether or not they are expert, I want to emphasize that one of the great privileges of my life has been to meet and talk with scores of professional individuals who hold this view, and virtually all are sincere. Over and over again, I have felt that when I'm with them, I am with Jesus. Even though they've come into evolutionary biology from other subdisciplines, they sincerely think that they have identified significant dents in the veracity of the discipline. To my recollection, I have never met a professional person opposed to evolution whom I have considered to be unintelligent. In virtually every case, what is driving them is their love for God and respect for the Bible as God's Word. They are definitely not idiots.

As for Todd, even if I've said it enough, I need to repeat it. Todd is one of the brightest persons I have ever met. I knew that was so from his extraordinary reputation but experienced it firsthand as we got to know each other. Despite our differences, as a couple of scientists, we speak the same language. In the early going, I was especially in awe to learn that he had been on the pioneering team in the massive project to sequence the rice genome. That's more than I can say for my own experience as a geneticist.

One of my favorite books of all time is *The Idiot* by Fyodor Dostoyevsky. The main character in the novel, the idiot, is a sort of Christ figure. Because of epileptic seizures, he has been unable to fit into Russian society and has been institutionalized, but for a little while he is out living in society, fitting into the sagas of life in Russia 150 years ago. He is really a very beautiful person, highly sympathetic to all of the various dilemmas that so powerfully affect the various protagonists as the story unfolds, and yet the power of evil and what it does to people deeply saddens him. He gets caught up in it all, giving himself to their sorrows, wanting to carry their burdens for them. The problems they bear do not seem trivial to him, despite the fact that he is supremely good and possesses a sort of otherworldly and remarkably mature form of wisdom. He is referred to as an idiot because of his seizures, and ultimately the social world of Russian society is too much for him as he is overcome by a seizure that takes him away once again.

The wisdom he possesses (perhaps brought about by his "other world" mental experiences) enables him to feel the pain of others, to love them despite their foibles, and to continually identify with them in the dilemmas they face. In Dostoyevsky's story, those who supposedly are the least idiotic, those who think they have things all sorted out, are the ones who are the real fools, because they seem to be unaware of just how ignorant they really are. It is the Prince (the "idiot" in the story) who has access to real wisdom.

In 1 Corinthians 1:20–24 Paul asks, "Where is the wise person? Where is the teacher of the law? Where is the philosopher of this age? Has not God made foolish the wisdom of the world? . . . Jews demand signs and Greeks look for wisdom, but we preach Christ crucified: a stumbling block to Jews and foolishness to Gentiles, but to those whom God has called, both Jews and Greeks, Christ the power of God and the wisdom of God."

There is a very real sense in which both Todd and I together are considered fools (idiots, I suppose) by many in the academic community. I have read scores of biology books about neurosciences, evolutionary biology, genetic engineering, and so on over the past several years. Those which discuss human origins almost without exception do so with the clear underlying assumption that humankind is present on earth as a result of a great cosmic accident. The view that there is something beyond the material, beyond what we can see and touch, is passe, they declare, a remnant, perhaps once evolutionarily advantageous, from deep in our past. Both Todd and I think along with Paul in his letter to the Colossians that "in him [Christ] all things were created: things in heaven and on earth" (1:16). We both believe that "he is before all things, and in him all things hold together" (1:17). We both believe that the Holy Spirit guides our lives, gives us strength and wisdom to live grounded in his love and his forgiveness. We believe in the power of prayer, that God hears millions of prayers being offered at exactly the same time and that we live and have our being in the Holy Spirit, who has chosen to live in us and through us. All of this is foolishness, idiocy even, to the majority of those in the academic world. But we stand together "convinced that neither death nor life, neither angels nor demons, neither the present nor the future, nor any powers, neither height nor depth, nor anything else in all creation, will be able to separate us from the love of God that is in Christ Jesus our Lord" (Rom. 8:38–39).

This does not mean that what we think about God's mechanism for creation is an insignificant detail. We each think that our opposing views are correct. One of us is wrong, and I am convinced it is Todd, just as he is convinced it is I. Ultimately it really matters to each of us that truth prevails, and we will work as long as we each live toward the establishment of truth as we see it in this regard. So although one of us is wrong about this matter, there is another much more important matter about which we are both right. It is that rightness—that righteousness, actually—in which we both stand. We stand together not through anything either of us has done—after all, we are both sinners redeemed and made right by God's grace—but rather as much-loved members of God's family. We are brothers of the same Lord (Heb. 2:11–12), and that makes all the difference.

────────── **For Study and Reflection** ──────────

1. While Darrel correctly acknowledges that neither he nor Todd is comfortable with derogatory terms such as "fool" and "heretic," he agrees that this type of rhetoric often accompanies disagreements. Regarding this

or other contentious topics (sexuality, prolife versus prochoice, immigration, etc.), what can you do to tone down the rhetoric?

2. Have you ever experienced a strained relationship with another Christian over a contentious issue, or are you aware of this happening? Why do you think it is so difficult for Christians to disagree without becoming antagonistic toward or dismissive of each other?

3. Why do you think some Christians would consider Darrel a heretic for accepting the theory of evolution? Do you think that is a fair characterization of him?

4. Darrel says that being "brothers of the same Lord" has contributed to his and Todd's ability to disagree vehemently over a serious issue, yet remain friends and treat each other with respect and kindness. In what ways could Christians who disagree be reminded that they are brothers and sisters of the same Lord?

5. Many Christians avoid talking about the things that divide them. What effect do you think this has on Christian unity?

6. Darrel and Todd still disagree on the topic of origins. Have they achieved unity or are they still divided? Explain.

WHAT HAVE WE ACCOMPLISHED?

Rob Barrett, The Colossian Forum

In the introduction, I noted that our culture is marked by an inability to bridge the divides between us. We disagree not just over issues but over ways of looking at the world. We commonly encounter people holding perspectives so different from our own that we just scratch our heads in wonder. We ask ourselves, "How in the world can they think that way?" Todd and Darrel decided to dive into that question. They weren't trying so much to win a debate (though both would like to) or to convince the other to abandon his view and switch sides (though that hope is always there). These remain secondary goals. Their primary goal was to pursue one another in love, knowing that they belong together as two parts of Christ's widely diverse body.

Some pages back, I quoted someone who turned down an invitation to join this project. He said that nothing positive could come from it. What do we say now, after spending many days during the course of a handful of years trying to do something positive? We said at the outset that we wanted to grow in truth and love. As we've journeyed together, we've regularly asked ourselves how we're doing. We've reflected on that question before God in prayer. What have we accomplished? What still needs to be done?

Sometimes it has been suggested that we've grown in love, but we're no closer to the truth. There's no question about that first part. Paul's great chapter on love in his letter to the Corinthians says, "Love is patient, love is kind. It does not envy, it does not boast, it is not proud. It does not dishonor others, it is not self-seeking, it is not easily angered, it keeps no record of wrongs. Love does not delight in evil but rejoices with the truth. It always protects, always trusts, always hopes, always perseveres. Love never fails" (1 Cor. 13:4–8). While we could all point to moments along the way when we contradicted those things, our time together and our relationships have been marked by these characteristics of love. This is more than being nice. It's more than agreeing to disagree. If we've spoken truly in these pages, perhaps you've gotten a glimpse of the kind of love we've seen.

Todd wrote about his concern for what Aunt Myrtle needs. She is not a scientist, a Bible scholar, or a theologian. Darrel doesn't want to damage her faith any more than Todd does. Quite the opposite, both want to bring her joy. The question is what these two can best offer as a faith-building gift to Aunt Myrtle. What if the most helpful thing for her isn't a coddling, simple answer about how to read Genesis but to observe an honest, loving struggle between Christians that demonstrates the truth of the gospel? Perhaps the thing that would encourage her most would be to see embodied love that rises above the ugly fighting that surrounds her every day.

I remember the start of one of our meetings. During the opening dinner, Todd had poured out a long list of difficulties he was facing. He felt alone and misunderstood. He was being attacked on multiple sides. As we walked from the restaurant to our hotel, Darrel made a point of walking beside him. I don't remember what Darrel said, but Todd just shook his head and asked, "What would my creationist friends say? I flew all the way here to be with Darrel Falk, the former president of BioLogos, so he could encourage me." Maybe the Aunt Myrtles of the world need to see some of this in the midst of all of the battles we seem to be fighting.

But what about the truth? Are we making any progress? I have to admit that Todd and Darrel are no closer to agreeing on the age of the earth than they were at our first meeting. There remains a giant gap between Todd's several thousand years and Darrel's several billion. If we limit our vision for growing in the truth to things like that, then no, we haven't accomplished much at all. But there's more to truth than that.

As part of that first tense meeting at the bed-and-breakfast, we invited a few dozen supporters of The Colossian Forum's work to gather and listen to Darrel, Todd, and the other attendees as they shared what had happened in their days together. We sent out the invitations before we knew the outcome. We were committed to honesty, so we agreed to share truthfully our successes and failures. No airbrushing of reality. As we began, we had no blockbuster revelations about reaching agreement on the big origins questions. But progress in the truth emerged nonetheless. Darrel affirmed that Todd was a knowledgeable scientist. He went so far as to say he thought Todd's research was legitimate and even valuable. The falsehood that Todd was foolish and ignorant gave way to the truth.

Todd stood in front of that group and said that he now knew that Darrel was a real Christian. He then went farther. He admitted that he had openly doubted Darrel's faith to others and that he owed them—and Darrel—an apology. He committed himself to righting that wrong.

The darkness of untruth was pushed a little farther back by the light of truth.

I remember one meeting where Todd said something inflammatory about Darrel and his friends. Some partisan evolutionists would have seethed silently and dashed off a message at the next break: "Creationist fool Todd Wood shows his true colors." But Darrel showed more Christian character than that. He paused to collect himself and quietly suggested, "I don't think you meant that. Would you like to try again?" Responses like this make space for the truth to come to light. Truth and love walk hand in hand.

After a couple of years of working with Todd, Darrel reflected on the difference this experience had made in his life. He talked about how engaging with Todd had helped him learn to bridge differences on other issues, even with his own family. He said, "This has been fun for me, because it's like a little experiment as to how Christianity is supposed to work." We gain something in both truth and love as this experiment continues.

Despite this sort of progress, we have to admit that we're still divided on the important origins issues. What do we say to that? Are we doomed to disagree forever?

In one meeting, Todd expressed his frustration at the deadlock. He had come to know that Darrel is a Christian, but then he said that this "makes it a thousand times more awkward, because I wonder why the God who convicts me for my position isn't convicting him. I don't know how to answer that question. So it leaves me uneasy." Darrel answered, "Like you, I puzzle a little bit: Why doesn't God sort things out for you and reveal truth to you in the way it seems he reveals it to me?"

Sorting this out will certainly require a miracle of God. But like many miracles, we are invited to play our part. Most miracles involve faithful people doing a lot of hard work at the same time. How might the miracle of reaching agreement about origins come to be?

My answer to that begins with describing what Darrel and Todd have accomplished, by the grace of God, so far. They started where we all start in these conflicts. They couldn't imagine how the other one was thinking. When we end up talking to such a person, our responses are largely governed by fear, distrust, and defensiveness. By God's grace, these two Christians were granted better instincts: love, trust, and vulnerability. As Darrel and Todd have lived out their calling, they have accomplished something unusual. They have gained an ability to ask an honest question and to attempt an honest answer. This is no small thing. To even understand the other's question requires learning a new language. To give an honest answer sometimes means admitting there are things you don't know.

What Darrel and Todd are doing is something like

foreign missions. They have met someone from a strange land and made friends. They have begun to learn their new friend's unusual ways. Like foreign travel, this has been simultaneously fascinating and uncomfortable. By getting to know a native, they can now speak more accurately about their friend and the way his people live. Not everyone can do this. To look at things through the eyes of another requires a certain confidence and peace that lets you enter into that foreign world without being afraid of losing yourself. Todd and Darrel have shown themselves able to do this. But this is only a first step.

To truly understand another culture and get past the "how can they possibly think that way?" barrier, you have to go live in that world. You can't just vacation there. If these two were to do that, the greater challenge probably would land on Darrel. He has not (yet) drunk deeply from the wells of young-earth creationism. Todd has trained and worked as a mainstream evolutionary biochemist. To really enter this other world, Darrel would need to cultivate Todd's habit of drawing scientific research hypotheses from his Bible reading. On the other side, Todd would need to learn what it is like to read Genesis 1–11 more poetically while yet holding on to the promise of resurrection.

It can be frightening to take off your shoes and walk in someone else's. What if you grow used to this place where they constantly drink in such harmful errors? Shouldn't we flee from evil rather than embrace it? Yes, it could be risky. But didn't Jesus reach out to those who were dangerously wrong? The people muttered about Jesus, "He has gone to be the guest of a sinner." Jesus responded, "The Son of Man came to seek and to save the lost" (Luke 19:7, 10). Jesus was unafraid of entering our dangerous, sinful world to help those he loved who were lost in error, even if it meant going to the cross. Who is willing to walk in Jesus' footsteps and go live with those who are lost in error about evolution?

To bridge the divide, we have to understand the other side from the viewpoint of an insider. We have to be able to speak the other's language, to see how their world works, and to see how it fails to work. Darrel and Todd have begun to blaze a trail, but they will make it only so far on their own. For one thing, their expertise lies in different subspecialties of evolutionary biology. It would take a lot of work to understand each other deeply, even if they were on the same side of this debate.

If we want to make real progress on these questions, it will require many people who are willing to cross the divide and live on the other side. Imagine a world where Todd's research is reviewed by someone in Darrel's circle. Todd's worst nightmare isn't that someone might call him a pseudoscientist. His greatest fear is that he might abandon good scientific practice and truly become a pseudoscientist out of his dogged pursuit of a scientific basis for creationism.

Darrel and his colleagues could help Todd be sure that he is asking legitimate questions, doing solid research, and drawing valid conclusions. Darrel could help protect Todd from becoming a fool. Likewise, Darrel doesn't want to stumble into thinking that the Bible is simply a collection of feel-good stories that aren't grounded in reality. Could Todd and his friends help Darrel avoid becoming a heretic? Todd regularly reminds us that God has always required his people to believe things that the world thinks are crazy. Darrel might need some help remembering this as he continues connecting his understanding of God to what he learns from science.

Darrel and Todd's journey together isn't the end of the story but a beginning. We at The Colossian Forum have a vision for Christians engaging our toughest differences in beautiful ways, filled with sacrificial love. We see this as the best pathway for getting to the truth. We also see it as a way of offering a gift to a world that has lost so much hope. If Christians have been given a ministry of reconciliation (2 Cor. 5:18), we couldn't live in a more opportune moment of history than these days of polarized conflict. The way of the cross and the resurrection offers a possibility for transforming our disagreements into something beautiful and true, filled with the kind of Holy Spirit breakthroughs these two friends of mine have experienced.

A second origins leader turned down our invitation to join this project. Like the first one I mentioned, he had spent a lot of time trying to engage those on the other side of the debate and he'd given up. He wrote to me, "I think the most fruitful way forward is to 'cut your losses.' . . . You just spin your wheels. You may achieve a slight turning down of the rhetoric and heat, but beyond that I don't see it being a good use of time. In other words, creationists and evolutionists can't 'work together.' They can be together, worship together, understand each other better, etc., but the underlying ideologies prevent truly working together."

From what I've seen in Darrel and Todd, I'm much more optimistic than this. At the same time, I can sympathize with this kind of discouragement. I've had times when I've wanted to cut my losses and give up too. But I think the world is dying to see the body of Christ working together across all of the many conflicts that try to divide us. Paul writes a beautiful description of what this would look like:

> So Christ himself gave the apostles, the prophets, the
> evangelists, the pastors and teachers, to equip his people

for works of service, so that the body of Christ may be built up until we all reach unity in the faith and in the knowledge of the Son of God and become mature, attaining to the whole measure of the fullness of Christ.

Then we will no longer be infants, tossed back and forth by the waves, and blown here and there by every wind of teaching and by the cunning and craftiness of people in their deceitful scheming. Instead, speaking the truth in love, we will grow to become in every respect the mature body of him who is the head, that is, Christ. From him the whole body, joined and held together by every supporting ligament, grows and builds itself up in love, as each part does its work.

—EPHESIANS 4:11–16

——— Your Colossians 1:17 Assignment ———

1. Who do you know and care about who holds a different view from your own about any important topic (for example, evolution, gun control, same-sex relationships/marriage, race, immigration, etc.)? Think about your friends and family.

2. Are you willing to try to understand them without attacking them? Dare you look at things through their eyes? If so, here are some questions you could ask:

a. What have you learned or experienced that led to your views about this topic?

b. What is at stake for you in this controversy? What are you concerned might happen when people get this wrong?

c. What concerns do you have about your own view on this topic?

d. How do your faith and your understanding of the Bible affect your views?

e. What do you think should be taught in school about this topic?

f. How would you like to see your church address this topic?

NOTES

Preface

1. G. K. Chesterton, *What's Wrong with the World* (1910; Mineola, NY: Dover Publications, 2007), 29.

Prologue

1. Jonathan P. Hill, "National Study of Religion and Human Origins" (2014), 8. Retrieved from https://biologos.org/uploads/projects/nsrho-report.pdf.
2. Pew Research Center, "Public's Views on Human Evolution" (December 30, 2013), 2. Retrieved from http://assets.pewresearch.org/wp-content/uploads/sites/11/2013/12/Evolution-12-30.pdf.
3. Pew Research Center, "Scientific Achievements Less Prominent Than a Decade Ago: Public Praises Science; Scientists Fault Public, Media" (July 9, 2009), 37. Retrieved from http://assets.pewresearch.org/wp-content/uploads/sites/5/legacy-pdf/528.pdf.
4. Karl W. Giberson, "2013 Was a Terrible Year for Evolution," *Daily Beast*, January 2, 2014. Retrieved from https://www.thedailybeast.com/2013-was-a-terrible-year-for-evolution.
5. National Academy of Sciences, *Science and Creationism: A View from the National Academy of Sciences*, 2nd ed. (Washington: National Academies Press, 1999), 25. Retrieved from https://www.nap.edu/read/6024/chapter/6.

6. The term "evolutionary creationist" is being used here and throughout this book to refer to a person who believes God created life on earth through an evolutionary process.

7. Edward J. Larson and Larry Witham, "Leading Scientists Still Reject God," *Nature* 394, no. 6691 (July 23, 1998): 313. Retrieved from https://www.nature.com/articles/28481 .pdf?origin=ppub.

8. John MacArthur, audio interview by Phil Johnson, "Evangelicals, Evolution, and the BioLogos Disaster," *Grace to You*, n.d. Retrieved from https://www.gty.org/ library/sermons-library/GTY136/evangelicals-evolution -and-the-biologos-disaster.

9. Pew Research Center, "Public's Views on Human Evolution," 2.

10. MacArthur, "Evangelicals, Evolution, and the BioLogos Disaster."

11. Ken Ham, "Christian Academics Telling God What He Got Wrong!" *Answers in Genesis*, January 25, 2014. Retrieved from https://answersingenesis.org/blogs/ ken-ham/2014/01/25/christian-academics-telling -god-what-he-got-wrong.

Chapter 1: Why Darrel Is Wrong and Why It Matters

1. I prefer the label "young-age creationist" to "young-earth creationist" because I believe more than the earth is young. This label indicates a belief that the entire creation (including the earth and the life on it) is only several thousand years old.

Chapter 2: Why Todd Is Wrong and Why It Matters

1. Russell Stannard, *Science and Wonders: Conversations about Science and Belief* (London: Faber and Faber, 1996), 13. Quoted with permission.

:iful World, Beautiful Savior

.dly curious about the mostly abandoned vapor
ry may wish to consult Joseph C. Dillow, *The
e: Earth's Pre-Flood Vapor Canopy* (Chicago:
;2), which is an adaptation of his earlier
i, Joseph C. Dillow, "Earth's Pre-Flood Vapor
ʾhD diss., Dallas Theological Seminary, 1978).
ɔn PAM matrices, see the original paper on their
ɔn: M. O. Dayhoff, R. M. Schwartz, and B. C.
. Model of Evolutionary Change in Proteins," in
ʾotein Sequence and Structure*, vol. 5 supp. 3, ed.
м. О. Dayhoff (Washington: National Biomedical Research
Foundation, 1978), 345–52.

Chapter 9: Overwhelming Evidence

1. Neil Shubin, *Your Inner Fish: A Journey into the 3.5-Billion-Year History of the Human Body* (New York: Pantheon, 2008).

2. For two clearly written summaries of the state of our current knowledge about human origins, see Ian Tattersall, *Masters of the Planet: The Search for Our Human Origins* (New York: St. Martin's Press, 2012), and Daniel Lieberman, *The Story of the Human Body: Evolution, Health, and Disease* (New York: Pantheon, 2013).

3. Darrel R. Falk, *Coming to Peace with Science: Bridging the Worlds between Faith and Science* (Downers Grove, IL: InterVarsity, 2004), 21.

4. For a thorough discussion of the way genetics provides evidence for evolution, see Graeme Finlay, *Human Evolution: Genes, Geneology, and Phylogenies* (Cambridge: Cambridge Univ. Press, 2013). For a more general discussion, see Francis Collins, *The Language of God: A Scientist Presents Evidence for Belief* (New York: Free Press, 2006).

5. Rachael is not this student's real name, and the story is a bit of a composite to ensure that I am not revealing confidential personal information that might be recognized by any former students.

6. Cited in Alister E. McGrath, *The Foundations of Dialogue in Science and Religion* (Oxford: Blackwell, 1998), 124.

Chapter 10: What about the Whales?

1. Technically, we wouldn't put them in a linear series per se, but rather we would recognize the Archaeoceti (fossil whales with hind legs) as "stem taxa" from the base of the evolutionary tree that describes the evolution of modern whales (the "crown taxa"). For more on whale evolution, see J. G. M. "Hans" Thewissen, *The Walking Whales: From Land to Water in Eight Million Years* (Los Angeles: Univ. of California Press, 2014).

2. For more on these cluster methods and how they are used in creation research, see Todd Charles Wood, "Visualizing Baraminic Distances Using Classical Multidimensional Scaling," *Origins* 57 (2005): 9–29; T. C. Wood, "Baraminology, the Image of God, and *Australopithecus sediba*," *Journal of Creation Theology and Science Series B: Life Sciences* 1 (2011): 6–14.

3. Much of my whale research is ongoing, but these results are described in S. R. Mace and T. C. Wood, "Statistical Evidence for Five Whale Holobaramins (Mammalia: Cetacea)," *Occasional Papers of the BSG* 5 (2005): 15.

4. David P. Cavanaugh, Todd C. Wood, and Kurt P. Wise, "Fossil Equidae: A Monobaraminic, Stratomorphic Series," in *Proceedings of the Fifth International Conference on Creationism*, ed. R. L. Ivey (Pittsburgh: Creation Science Fellowship, 2003), 143–53.

5. My most recent results on hominins are found in T. C.
   Wood, "An Evaluation of *Homo naledi* and 'Early *Homo*' from
   a Young-Age Creationist Perspective," *Journal of Creation
   Theology and Science Series B: Life Sciences* 6 (2016): 14–30.
6. For example, Todd Charles Wood, "Animal and Plant
   Baramins," *CORE Issues in Creation* 3 (2008): 1–258. See
   also Todd Charles Wood, "*Natura Facit Saltum*: The Case for
   Discontinuity," *CORE Issues in Creation* 5 (2009): 113–27.
7. John H. Whitmore, Guy Forsythe, and Paul A. Garner,
   "Intraformational Parabolic Recumbent Folds in the
   Coconino Sandstone (Permian) and Two Other Formations
   in Sedona, Arizona (USA)," *Answers Research Journal* 8
   (2015): 21–40; John Whitmore, Raymond Strom, Stephen
   Cheung, and Paul A. Garner, "The Petrology of the
   Coconino Sandstone (Permian), Arizona, USA," *Answers
   Research Journal* 7 (2014): 499–532.
8. For example, Stephen P. Cheung, Raymond Strom, John H.
   Whitmore, and Paul A. Garner, "Occurrence of Dolomite
   Beds, Clasts, Ooids and Unidentified Microfossils in the
   Coconino Sandstone, Northern Arizona," *Geological Society of
   America Abstracts with Programs* 41 (2009): 119; Paul A. Garner
   and John H. Whitmore, "What Do We Know about Marine
   Sand Waves? A Review of Their Occurrence, Morphology
   and Structure," *Geological Society of America Abstracts with
   Programs* 43 (2011): 596; John H. Whitmore, Guy Forsythe,
   Raymond Strom, and Paul A. Garner, "Unusual Bedding Styles
   for the Coconino Sandstone (Permian), Arizona," *Geological
   Society of America Abstracts with Programs* 43 (2011): 433.

Interlude 5: Beyond Disagreement

1. Augustine, *On Christian Doctrine*, book 1, chapter 36.
2. Ibid.

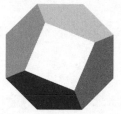

THE
COLOSSIAN
FORUM™
Hope in Practice

The Colossian Forum equips leaders to transform cultural conflicts into opportunities for spiritual growth and witness. Our vision: a Christian community that acts Christian, *especially* in the face of conflict.

Visit **www.ColossianForum.org** for more information.

Rob Barrett (PhD [applied physics], Stanford University; and PhD [theology], Durham University [UK]) is director of forums and scholarship at The Colossian Forum. Rob has numerous publications in fields ranging from biblical studies to physics, data storage technology, and human-computer interaction. His varied background is unified by his longstanding interest in the intersection of faith, Bible, science/technology, and culture.